## Resources Series

Sugar

# Sugar

BEN RICHARDSON

polity

First published in 2015 by Polity Press

Polity Press
65 Bridge Street
Cambridge CB2 1UR, UK

Polity Press
350 Main Street
Malden, MA 02148, USA

ISBN-13: 978-0-7456-8014-9
ISBN-13: 978-0-7456-8015-6(pb)

A catalogue record for this book is available from the British Library.

Richardson, Ben, 1982-
  Sugar / Ben Richardson.
      pages cm
  Includes bibliographical references and index.
  ISBN 978-0-7456-8014-9 (hardback : alk. paper) -- ISBN 978-0-7456-8015-6
(pbk. : alk. paper)  1.  Sugar trade.  I. Title.
  HD9100.5.R527 2015
  382'.456641--dc23
                                              2015009365
Typeset in 10.5 on 13pt Scala by
Servis Filmsetting Ltd, Stockport, Cheshire
Printed and bound in the UK by Clays Ltd, St Ives plc

The publisher has used its best endeavours to ensure that the URLs for external websites referred to in this book are correct and active at the time of going to press. However, the publisher has no responsibility for the websites and can make no guarantee that a site will remain live or that the content is or will remain appropriate.

Every effort has been made to trace all copyright holders, but if any have been inadvertently overlooked the publisher will be pleased to include any necessary credits in any subsequent reprint or edition.

For further information on Polity, visit our website:
politybooks.com

# Contents

# Acknowledgements

My obsession with sugar started in 2005 when I began my PhD on the political economy of the international sugar trade. This was generously funded by the UK Economic and Social Research Council, as was the following post-doctoral research on the investment strategies of transnational sugar companies. One post-doc wasn't enough, so I applied for another to look at how the livelihoods of the rural poor were being affected by the sugar industry and assess how these people might be better protected. This research was funded by the Leverhulme Trust Early Career Fellowship scheme.

All in all, I have been fortunate enough to conduct interviews in Belgium, Brazil, the Dominican Republic, India, Swaziland, Switzerland, Trinidad, the United Kingdom, the United States of America, and Zambia. Sugar is truly a global commodity. I am incredibly grateful to all these interviewees and to the research councils for funding me.

This book brings together the research I have conducted during the last ten years and in so doing benefits from the co-authors I have worked with along the way. The list has become long: Tony Heron, James Brassett, William Smith, Pamela Richardson-Ngwenya, Elizabeth Fortin, João Nunes, Ben McKay, Sérgio Sauer, Roman Herre, Liam Campling, James Harrison, Adrian Smith and Natasha Schwarzbach. Natasha and the rest of the Bonsucro Secretariat, along with Olivier Genevieve of Ethical Sugar, have also been extremely helpful in providing me with contacts, advice and encouragement as I have gone about my research.

I have also been tremendously lucky to work in the Department of Politics and International Studies at the University of Warwick, which has been a vibrant source of ideas and support. Special mention goes to my mentor Matthew Watson, to the members of the International Political Economy research cluster, and to Tim Sinclair, Ben Clift and Sarah Wallace for commenting on draft chapters.

On this note, I want to pay sincere thanks to the two anonymous reviewers who read the whole manuscript and made really detailed and helpful suggestions. I think the book is much improved because of them. Likewise, a big thank you goes to Louise Knight and Pascal Porcheron at Polity for giving me the chance to write the book and then steering me through to completion.

Last but not least is my loving wife Katy. She has been there for me throughout this period and made my life so much sweeter. I would like to dedicate this book to her.

CHAPTER ONE

# Introduction

The global food system has produced a paradox: the world population is simultaneously stuffed and starved. Figures from 2013 show that two billion people are deficient in micronutrients, 868 million have inadequate calorie intake, and 500 million are exposed to diet-related disease because of excessive weight gain.[1] Yet although these manifestations of malnutrition might be embodied in different ways, they are increasingly symptomatic of the same experiences of poverty and discrimination. It is these underlying social inequalities that account for the maldistribution of food and which are perpetuated by the very way in which the food system functions.[2] This is no accident, of course. For all the harm it has caused, the paradox of food has been good for profits.

A study of sugar has much to tell us about this situation. On the one hand, the way sugar production is organized has denied millions of people the means to buy or grow enough food to feed themselves. The reasons for their poverty differ. Workers have been exploited through low wages or made redundant by mechanization, farmers have been indebted or marginalized in favour of large landowners, and rural dwellers have lost livelihood opportunities or been squeezed off their land. Yet the end result has been the same. Vulnerable people have not received a fair share of the wealth produced by the sugar industry, and, in some cases, have actually been harmed by its more rapacious practices. On the other hand, many of the so-called junk foods that constitute poor-quality diets contain added sugar and other sweeteners. By changing the taste of products and engaging in extensive marketing campaigns, food manufacturers and retailers have been able to transform dietary habits, reorganizing patterns of consumption on a global scale. Average sugar intake more than quadrupled during the twentieth century, with levels of obesity and diabetes following close behind.[3]

This book seeks to explain these dynamics and explore their injustices. It does so largely with respect to the sweetener made from sugar cane and sugar beet, namely sucrose. While other sweeteners such as high fructose corn syrup can be commonly found in foods and drinks, sucrose remains by far the world's most popular added sugar. Focusing on cane/beet sugar rather than the entire gamut of dietary sugars is helpful for a number of reasons. Sucrose, especially in its 'pure' isolated form as refined sugar, is understood as being qualitatively different from other sugars, such as lactose sugar present in milk. For this reason, when thinking about its effects on health, it is useful to distinguish it from other sources of sweetness.

Centring on a specific commodity also makes it easier to trace it back through the supply chain. This allows us to link questions about consumption to those concerning exchange and production. This is important because, as suggested in the paragraph above, the politics of sugar are to be found in its supply as well as in its demand.

Finally, making the connections between consumption and production also encourages us to take a more global perspective, since many of the supply chains which characterize the contemporary food system operate across national borders. Not only does this perspective give us the bigger picture, it also takes us to parts of the world where sugar is treated very differently and thereby illuminates alternative ways in which the commodity can be understood.

This book, then, is not solely about what we eat but also about how we live. In this sense, though the object of the study is narrow, the question asked is deliberately broad: *how are social relations remade through sugar?*

It is the relations of inequality perpetuated through the daily practices of individuals consuming, exchanging and producing sugar that we are particularly interested in. One example can be found in oral health since tooth decay is closely linked to sugary foods. Because of differences in diet and dental treatment borne out over a lifetime, the poorest people in England end up with five fewer teeth than the richest.[4] The imprint of sugar upon people's mouths can thus be read as both a manifestation and a marker of their social status.

Such inequalities are not solely down to differences in class. Hierarchies based on gender, age, race, ethnicity, caste and nationality are equally important and frequently intersect at the individual level. For instance, because of the different ways their work is valued, the female worker cultivating sugar cane in India earns much less than her male counterpart sowing sugar beet in Germany. It is the ambition of this book to chart these intersecting inequalities and introduce to the reader the fate of those people purposely distanced from the seductive world of sweetness and light portrayed in industry marketing materials. This is the bitter side of sugar, and one worth knowing.

## The global politics of sugar: the limits of existing approaches

Existing studies of sugar typically fall into one of two camps. The first camp deals with the poverty-inducing effects of sugar and tends to frame it as an issue of international trade. This results from the curious situation whereby exactly the same product, refined sugar or pure sucrose, can be made from two entirely different crops. These are the grass-crop sugar cane which is grown in tropical climates and the root-crop sugar beet which is grown in temperate climates. The near-universal ability to grow sugar crops has thus allowed governments across the world to build up a domestic sugar industry by protecting markets from imports and supporting producers with favourable prices.

The legacies of this are extensive. There are an estimated 1.1 million jobs in sugar manufacturing and tens of millions more in sugar farming scattered across more than 120 countries.[5] By contrast, coffee production takes place in sixty countries and cocoa production in just thirty. Furthermore, sugar is considered by the World Bank to be the second most protected agricultural commodity in the world behind rice. In 2008, the level of import tariffs and domestic subsidies on sugar accounted for almost one-fifth of all agricultural support – that amounts to a lot of redistributive tax.[6] The injustice that both free traders and development campaigners have pointed out is that protectionist policies have largely benefited sugar-beet producers in developed countries. They argue that, by keeping out sugar-cane exports from developing countries, trade barriers have denied poor people the chance to trade their way out of poverty and thus confined them to a life of hunger. Or as the *Wall Street Journal* once pithily put it: 'Addiction to sugar subsidies chokes poor nations' exports.'[7]

While trade protection remains important in shaping who benefits from sugar production, the idea that the industry is controlled by wealthy farmers in Europe and the United States of America is increasingly untenable. First, significant steps towards liberalization have happened over

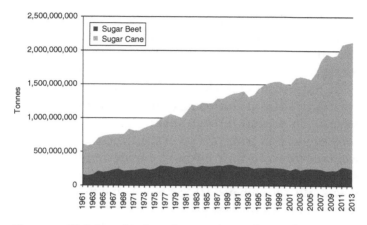

Figure 1.1 Global production of sugar cane and sugar beet, 1961–2013

*Source*: FAOSTAT

the last two decades, turning the European Union into a net sugar importer for the first time since the 1970s and opening up the United States to unlimited imports from Mexico. In fact, the United States is consistently one of the world's biggest importers of sugar.

Second, most of the extra demand for sugar crops has come from Asia, Africa and Latin America – not just to make sugar but biofuel too – meaning that production has increased most rapidly in these regions. This is made clear in Figure 1.1. In 1961, just over a quarter of the total sugar crop harvest was made up of sugar beet, but, by 2013, this had fallen to less than one-eighth. The majority of the world's sugar that year was produced by Brazil, India, China and Thailand, the powerhouses of the global sugar economy.

The third problem with the trade protectionism argument is an analytical one. A major weakness of many studies of the international sugar trade is the way they have

treated countries as homogeneous units rather than hierar-
chical societies. Since there is significant inequality *within*
countries as well as *between* them, focusing on which country sugar is produced in only gives us part of the picture.

There are many examples of non-farming men (and they
are usually men) in developing countries who have become
fantastically wealthy through sugar while their fellow citizens languish in poverty. Two of the richest people in the
world in fact built their business empires on the back of
sugar-trading enterprises: the Nigerian Aliko Dangote,
now worth an estimated US$25 billion and the Malaysian
Robert Kuok worth US$12 billion. Others have found their
fortunes as industrialists. The Brazilian Rubens Ometto
Silveria Mello, worth US$2 billion, made his money at the
helm of a sugar-cane milling company and was dubbed by
Forbes 'the world's first ethanol billionaire'.

And nor is it just among the elites of Africa, Asia
and Latin America that colossal sugar fortunes can be
found. There are the Fanjul brothers who own Florida
Crystals Corporation and American Sugar Refining, the
Weston family which owns AB Sugar and its parent company Associated British Foods, and the Russian Vadim
Moshkovich who owns Russia's biggest sugar and agricultural holding company Rusagro. And beyond those
businesses selling sugar as an ingredient, there are those
*re*selling it in the form of manufactured foods and drinks.
These include western-based multinational corporations
like Coca-Cola, Hershey's, Kellogg's, Mars, Mondelez,
Nestlé, PepsiCo and Unilever. Together, these companies made over US$50 billion *profit* in 2013 – a handsome
return for their shareholders.[8] These individual and organizational examples of wealth accumulation all belie the idea
that we can determine who benefits from sugar simply by
looking at national levels of output and export.

The other camp of sugar studies is concerned with its adverse health effects. If the injustices of sugar production have been framed as a problem of trade protectionism, then those relating to consumption have been framed, quite separately, as a problem of corporate manipulation. Part of this manipulation stems from the fact that vast amounts of money are spent marketing foods high in sugar, salt and fat so that consumers are simply barraged into buying more of these products. Another part stems from the activities of the food industry in shaping the official information given to consumers. This comes in the form of dietary guidelines and on-product labels, many of which are government approved and so require extensive lobbying to shape. According to the critics, this political manipulation allows the big corporations to make their products *appear* healthier than they really are. Taken together, the food industry is charged with purposely misleading the public into dangerous eating habits.

One need only look at the list of books on sugar to see how appealing this argument has become. In 2013–14 alone, there was *Fat Chance: The Hidden Truth about Sugar, Obesity and Disease* by Robert Lustig; *Sugar Nation: The Hidden Truth behind America's Deadliest Habit and the Simple Ways to Beat It* by Jeff O'Connell; and *Salt, Sugar, Fat: How the Food Giants Hooked Us* by Michael Moss. Like the literature on trade protectionism though, while it contains some important insights, as a political critique this approach also has its limitations.[9]

First, it tends to ignore the countervailing appeal of books, television shows and magazine articles promoting all manner of fad diets and detoxes. Among these are Atkins, Dukan, glycaemic index, paleo and No Sugar, all of which have changed the consumption of sugar either by discriminating against sucrose or by shifting eating habits away from sweetened foods altogether. Studies which focus only on the power wielded by 'food giants' risk missing how these companies are responding to market and regulatory pressures by reformulating products using artificial sweeteners and changing their image by buying up health-conscious brands (although, as we will see in chapter 2, this is by no means a solution to the spread of diet-related disease).

Second, these studies are divorced from issues of production, which limits our understanding of what is happening at the farm level and poses questions about the supply of sugar. Indeed, while the literature on trade complains about sugar being too expensive because of protectionism, the literature on consumption complains about its ubiquity and concludes it must be too cheap! The supply of sugar is not only complicated by the different values people attach to its price. Sugar cane and sugar beet can be put to a range of uses: once the sucrose-rich juice has been squeezed out of the crop, it can be crystallized and refined for food or fermented and distilled for fuel. One of the biggest developments in recent years has been the growth of the sugar fuel market. By 2013, fully 15 per cent of global sugarcane production was turned into biofuel, a proportion which is expected to almost double over the next decade.[10] Meanwhile, the masses of corn grown in the United States diverted into biofuel production have put inflationary pressure on the price of high fructose corn syrup (HFCS), a competitor to sugar used mainly in soft drinks. Looking only at the food market thus misses a big part of the story about how agricultural crops are used, priced and regulated.

Third, the account blaming corporations for unfolding health epidemics tends to be based on the experience of the United States. Given that each country has a unique mix of characteristics – in this case an influential state agricultural

department close to agribusiness and an ideological climate conditioned by individualism – we should be cautious
about generalizing any findings to the rest of the world.
Unfortunately, analyses of the American food industry are
often just transplanted, rather than translated into other
national contexts. Related to this, and perhaps as a result
of their focus on sugar consumption and corporate manipulation, these accounts also have little to say about the
prospects for conscious political change. For example, in
his otherwise excellent book, the journalist Michael Moss
concludes by putting his faith in enlightened shopping to
save the day. In his closing paragraph, he argues that 'They
[the major food corporations] may have salt, sugar and fat
on their side, but, we, ultimately, have the power to make
choices. After all, we decide what to buy. We decide how
much to eat.'[11]

Not only is this a perverse conclusion to reach after spend-
ing the previous 346 pages detailing the myriad ways that
American consumers have virtually no meaningful choice
over what they eat, it also rules out other sources of change
and ways of acting. Where are the political parties responding to voters, the state agencies protecting the public, the
campaign groups formed by citizens and the social movements reshaping values? By reducing politics to individual
choice at the checkout and starving it of its collective character and varied institutional expression, accounts like the one
given by Moss may do more harm than good.

## The approach and argument

So how should the global politics of sugar be approached
instead? This book proceeds from two foundations. The
first is that the circulation of sugar is deeply structured by
global capitalism. In the early 1990s, there were a series of

seismic events which entrenched and extended capitalism on a worldwide scale: the dissolution of the planned economies of the Union of Soviet Socialist Republics (USSR); the surging of foreign investment in coastal China; the integration of European Union members into a single market; and the liberalization of international trade through the North American Free Trade Agreement and the formation of the World Trade Organization. All of these fundamentally changed the way that sugar is produced, exchanged and consumed, and it is important to cast a critical eye upon these developments, rather than accept them as the inevitable or benign progress of history.

To develop such a critique does not mean advocating Communist revolution of the food system, though the idea is certainly intriguing (Eaters of the world, unite. You have nothing to lose but your fast-food chains!). Rather, it means providing an analysis of capitalism which centres on the inequalities and contradictions caused by the ceaseless pursuit of profit. We have already mentioned some of the social inequalities perpetuated through sugar in the form of tooth decay and pittance wages. Others will emerge when we consider how capital accumulation takes advantage of other forms of underpaid work and free gifts from nature at various places around the world.

Similarly, we have also noted one of the contradictions shaped by sugar, namely the tendency of capitalism to undermine the basis of its own survival, in this case by making healthy people ill. Like other contradictions we will look at, such as the overproduction of sugar leading to periodic market crashes, these have led to crises (an obesity crisis, a farm crisis) which state authorities have sought to manage. And contrary to the common assertion that equates capitalism with free markets, what a critical study of sugar reveals is that capitalists themselves have called for state intervention, either to make a market function in their interests or else protect them from the vagaries of it.

At the same time as taking global capitalism seriously, it is also important not to ascribe to it uniform and omnipresent characteristics. This is the book's second foundation: that capitalism need not be a single fate.[12] This refers both to the different ways in which capitalist economies can be organized (compare the United States with France, for example) and to the limits to which capitalist principles of private property, commodification and endless accumulation extend. Just in relation to sugar, we might think of the bake-a-cake sales that raise money for charity. This is not a vulgar profit-oriented pursuit but is a valid way in which resources are distributed and social ends attained through the exchange of sweetened food for money.

What this second foundation does, then, is to create some room for human agency. Without this the analysis would be very deterministic, with every eventuality reduced to the inner workings of capital (other accounts of sugar have been equally guilty of determinism, ascribing everything to its irresistible sweetness or the characteristics of cane).[13] So in this respect we try to be a little bit like the female slave in Grace Nichols's famous poem 'Sugar Cane', who recognizes that, for all the power accorded to the mystical King Sugar in the colonies of the Caribbean, 'it is us who groom and weed him, who stick him in the earth in the first place.'[14] Likewise, one of the key messages of the book is that the current sugar system is a product of human choice and should not be naturalized . Moreover, whether it is through health professionals, state elites, organized labour or social activists, there are a multitude of actors capable of challenging this settlement. It is we who make the meaning of sugar, and we who can un-make it too.

This brings us to the book's central argument, which is that progressive political change is not about changing people's relationship to sugar per se but about changing our relationships to one another. For instance, reducing sugar consumption may lower some people's risk of diabetes, but if those same people remain reliant on poor-quality food, then it is likely that they will suffer from other forms of diet-related ill-health instead. Similarly, increasing the yield of sugar crops may help farmers make a decent living, but only in so far as they are not then subject to price cuts by other businesses in the supply chain.

These changes in social relations come about through site-specific struggles to value life differently. They are site-specific because they take different forms in different places – a campaign against child advertising here, a protest against water pollution there. But what they have in common is a desire to govern by a different metric, one that recognizes values beyond 'the bottom line', be it the sanctity of childhood or the preservation of the environment. At its furthest reaches, the book therefore hints at how these contestations might cohere into broader systemic change that would make sugar provisioning more ecologically sound and socially just.

## Historicizing sugar and rethinking politics

The common story to tell about sugar traces the westward travel of sugar-cane plants from their native habitats in South Asia. The first known human cultivation of sugar cane was in New Guinea at least 6,000 years ago, where it was chewed for its sweetness and used as animal fodder. The practice of crushing and boiling the sucrose-rich juice into a sweet viscous mass then developed in the wider region, with the first records of crystallized sugar located in India in 500 BC, used, it seems, for medicinal purposes. From here, plant varieties and production techniques spread to China, Persia and, carried by Arabs, reached the Mediterranean basin by 700 AD.

Cultivation of these exotic plants, known rather beautifully as 'reeds that produce honey without bees', continued under Christian rule before spreading to the Atlantic Islands where it became bound up for the first time with European colonialism. Sugar cane was carried by Columbus from the Spanish Canaries to the New World in 1493, from where it went to the Caribbean and then to Brazil. By 1625, the Portuguese were supplying nearly all of Europe with sugar from Brazil through refining centres in Lisbon, Antwerp and Amsterdam.

Early sugar production in the Americas represented a transitional stage in the evolution of sugar production. While the size of the sugar-cane estates began to rise, the planting and processing techniques were essentially no different from those inherited from the Arabs. It was not until 1650 that the Caribbean began to produce significant amounts of sugar for export, due to English planting, first in Barbados and later in Jamaica, and French planting in Saint-Domingue (modern-day Haiti). These islands were the epicentre of what became known as 'the sugar revolution' – a transformation to absentee owners, slave-based gang labour, intensive monoculture plantations, faster cane-crushing technologies and bulk long-distance trade that had far-reaching consequences. In the words of historian Elizabeth Abbott, it was the moment that 'Much like oil today, sugar [became] the most powerful commodity on earth.'[15]

While the sugar-cane frontier continued to cycle through the Americas during the nineteenth century, overseen by the government of the now-independent United States, a competitor crop was taking hold in continental Europe. In 1747, a German chemist, Andreas Marggraf, had found a way to make crystallized sugar from a specially bred variety of beet. Hugely inefficient at the outset, the embryonic sugar-beet industry was given the support it needed during the Napoleonic Wars (1803–1815) when Britain's blockade of Europe interrupted the supply of Caribbean sugar to the continent, leading governments to stimulate domestic production through subsidies. Aided further by the abolition of slavery and British trade liberalism, which together made the sugar-beet industry more competitive in the large British import market, European sugar production grew considerably. Indeed, by the 1890s, Germany was producing more sugar than the entire Caribbean.

At the same time, on the other side of the world, the plantation model pioneered in Barbados continued to spread, helping sugar cane to complete its circumnavigation of the globe. Export zones in the colonial territories of the Philippines, Taiwan and Java took off, driven largely by demand in the industrializing areas of China and Japan. Meanwhile, complementing the older Atlantic trade circuits, European colonialists also established plantations in Mauritius and Natal on the Indian Ocean, and Fiji and Queensland on the Pacific Ocean, worked by indentured labour brought from India and – to bring the story of sugarcane cultivation full circle – New Guinea also. Thus, by the end of the nineteenth century, as the geographer Jack Galloway affirms, the production of sugar for food consumption had become 'one of the major economic activities of the entire tropical world'.[16]

During the first half of the twentieth century, the contradictions of this voracious enterprise reached breaking point. Export prices routinely became so low that sugar producers exposed to these markets were threatened with extinction. This led to ambitious international agreements to try and control prices. Following outbreaks of war and economic depression, state management deepened further as domestic stabilization policies over national sugar markets were enacted. The 1932 Sugar Protection Act in India, the 1934 Jones–Costigan Act in the United States, the establishment of the British Sugar Corporation in 1936 and Japanese control of Taiwanese production signalled the new lengths that states would go to guarantee supplies of sugar. The reluctance to rely on free trade also meant that, by the end of the 1940s, just 10 per cent of all sugar consumed was acquired on the 'open' world market, the rest remaining within national markets or exchanged through preferential trade agreements.

There were also political convulsions wrought by the glaring disparities of wealth. In the 1910s, Emiliano Zapata led revolutionary peasants to reclaim land from the sugarcane *haciendas* in Mexico, in the 1930s black sugar workers in Jamaica went on strike against their colonial employers, and in the 1950s discontent in Cuba's sugar industry helped build support for Fidel Castro's overthrow of the Batista dictatorship. The subsequent embargo placed on Cuban exports by the United States and the nationalization of American-owned land and sugar mills in Cuba was the major story of the 1960s as the international sugar trade realigned with Cold War politics. Another part of this story was the export of American corn to Japan and South Korea as part of their anti-Communist geopolitical pact, which from the 1970s initiated the mass consumption of high fructose corn syrup in Asia.

Among the newly independent colonies of European empire, those that did not already produce sugar began to invest in domestic processing or refining facilities, often using European capital and contractors. For example, as part of their strategic reorientation from direct ownership to investment and trade services, the British companies Tate & Lyle and Booker McConnell advised on more than fifty sugar projects in Africa during the 1970s. By the end of the 1980s, domestic sugar or sweetener industries had been established in almost every country in the world, from Albania to Zambia. The way sugar was governed would now be of universal concern.

Although this book is focused on the contemporary politics of sugar and will largely confine itself to the period 1995–2015, there are many ways in which it has been informed by historical study and the alternative ways of thinking about sugar politics that this throws up. Three examples are briefly outlined.

The first use of history is to see things from a different perspective. As we shall see in chapter 2, there is much debate at present about applying taxes to sweetened products in order to tackle obesity. Many opponents of this, like writers at the free market Adam Smith Institute in the United Kingdom, have argued that this kind of state intervention is neither effective nor ethical: 'what we eat and drink is simply no one's business but our own,' they say.[17] Consulting the historical record, we find that many of these debates have in fact been held before. Indeed, Adam Smith himself weighed in on the issue of taxing sugar in the common interest in his famous 1776 book, *The Wealth of Nations*. In this, he wrote that 'Sugar, rum and tobacco are commodities which are nowhere necessaries of life, which are become objects of almost universal consumption, and which are therefore extremely proper subjects of taxation.'[18] Although he proposed this as a means to raise revenue for Britain's bankrupt empire rather than improve the health of the nation, Smith's reflections on the legitimacy of taxing sugar are surely still relevant today, not least for liberal commentators invoking his name.

We could go even further with Smith's ideas on sugar. For example, his division of commodities into necessaries and luxuries raises questions not just about the taxation of sugar but about its basic social utility. Today, we often hear how the world has to produce more food to feed a growing population. If, like Smith, we also consider sugar a luxury, we might well ask if the resources used to grow sugar cane and sugar beet would not be better turned over to the production of staples like grains and vegetables instead. Given that one-fifth of the total sugar-cane and -beet harvest is used for non-food purposes (i.e. biofuel) and the rest turned into so much sugar that the total supply far exceeds what most public health officials recommend, should be consumed as a whole, it seems a question well worth asking.

The second use of historical research relates to the lived experience of sugar. Let us take the transatlantic slave trade as an example. In this trade, it is reckoned that 11 million slaves were transported to the Americas between 1519 and 1867, mainly from West Africa.[19] The legacies of this are extensive, seen in systems of racism, Africanized cultures and unequal landholdings, among other things. This might be considered ancient history, but, on some occasions, the activities of the colonial sugar industry have once again become live political issues.

One such occasion was in 2014 when a representative of the Caribbean Community, Sir Hilary Beckles, made his case for reparations to be paid by European countries for the suffering inflicted by the transatlantic slave trade. Speaking in the UK parliament, Sir Hilary noted that when the British government abolished slavery, instead of compensating the enslaved workers of the Caribbean they in fact indemnified slave-owners for the loss of their human property. The plantation owners were paid £47 million, about £4 billion in today's money. Worse still, half of this was paid by emancipated slaves themselves in the form of a compulsory four-year period of free labour known as apprenticeship. Nowadays, the Caribbean Community views this act of the British as a flat denial of responsibility and an ongoing injustice in world affairs. Therefore, their demands were for European governments to provide a formal apology for slavery and support reconciliation measures. Among these were repatriation of those Afro-Caribbean people who wished to return to their homeland and medical assistance for the hypertension and diabetes pandemic in the Caribbean which, in their words, 'is the direct result of the nutritional experience ... associated with slavery, genocide and apartheid'.[20]

That same year, 2014, the Atlantic sugar trade was also being debated in the United States, though prompted by a very different kind of intervention. In a disused sugar refinery in New York, the artist Kara Walker had installed a giant female sphinx with a twist – a black woman coated in 160,000 pounds of refined white sugar (Figure 1.2). With its deliberately racialized features, the sphinx sparked much reflection. Did the sphinx's maidservant kerchief, bare breasts and inflated buttocks reinforce negative stereotypes of the Afro-American woman, or did it recast her in a new position of power? Was the artwork a lament about the closure of the sugar refinery and the factory jobs it provided to black workers or a critique of the continued bodily damage wrought by sugar on the black population in the form of diet-related disease? Whatever the answers reached, it was evident that the lived history of sugar still remains relevant to the way identity and exploitation could be collectively understood.

The final use of history is to illuminate alternative forms

Figure 1.2 A Subtlety by Kara Walker

of provisioning. When thinking about the contemporary political economy of sugar, it is tempting to take much of what we see as fixed and immutable: for example, that sugar is used as a sweetener. Arguably, many of the assumptions made in this way are a result of the reliance on western histories, the 'common story of sugar' referred to previously. Yet, as histories of India have shown, lumps of unrefined sugar have also been used in medicinal treatments, ceremonial offerings and as a currency to pay for village services or to settle debt. The sucrose in the plant itself has also been used differently, kept in its juice form and taken directly as a drink. This is important as it can help us imagine alternative ways in which the crop might be configured as something other than a commodified food ingredient.

Studies of sugar in Asia also show the different ways in which production has been organized. As detailed by the historian Ulbe Bosma,[21] although British and Dutch colonialists wanted to replicate the Atlantic plantation model in India and Java, they were unable to orchestrate the sweeping transformations that had characterized the Caribbean and so had to adopt a different approach. What resulted was the 'Asian plantation'. For Bosma, this rested on an alliance between the European sugar mill owners and indigenous landholding elites, with the latter used to coerce peasants into growing cane and to organize the agricultural workforce. This model continues to condition sugar production in these regions today. As we shall see in chapter 4, even in some sugar industries supposedly based on smallholder production, a class of farmers can be found who have come to control the supply of sugar cane and effectively turn other villagers into labourers on their own land.

These alternative accounts are useful for more than just imagining other ways of using and producing sugar. They can also provide us with different ideas of political agency and cultural politics. For instance, the historian Seymour Drescher has written on the female-dominated crowd in the Paris riots in 1792, which reacted to the rising price of sugar by launching a *taxation populaire*, seizing sugar from traders accused of hoarding and selling it in public at the traditional 'just price'.[22] This was very different from the campaign of abstention pursued by female sugar consumers in Britain around the same time, but in similar fashion showed the potential for change to emerge outside the political establishment and within civil society instead. The existence of the current fair trade movement, for instance, owes much to the feminized abolitionism of the late eighteenth century, evident in its heartfelt appeal to the buying public based on sympathy towards a distant other.

Figure 1.3 Sugar-cane monoculture

On cultural politics, meanwhile, Michael Niblett has illustrated the way that the sugar frontier has been registered in the literary texts of Caribbean writers. In these texts, the rapid socio-ecological changes wrought by world market fluctuations and monoculture seasonality have often been attributed to an autonomous King Sugar, a restless cane which contrives to author its own story. This aesthetic representation of sugar – what Niblett has dubbed 'saccharine irrealism' – suggests how people at the sugar-cane frontier in the Global South today might be experiencing its strange new rhythms of boom and bust.[23] Certainly, the description of sugar-cane plantations by peasant women in Brazil as 'green deserts' of monoculture encroaching on their homeland would seem to chime with this.[24]

Taken together, what these examples show is that the history of sugar can do more than simply serve as a backdrop to current events. By showing the contingent and contested way in which things were brought about in the past, we can better think how things in the present might change or be reappraised. While this book focuses on the current historical juncture of sugar, it does so with this critical apparatus firmly in mind.

It is organized in the following way. After the Introduction, chapter 2 looks at the consumption of sugar and the relationship between its intrinsic sweetness, on the one hand, and the meaning attributed to sugar-sweetened foods, on the other hand. It is argued that to better understand why sugar is consumed the way it is, we cannot simply refer to its chemical properties but need also to appreciate the way in which taste is socialized, eating understood and food provided. Chapter 3 then looks at international trade relations and the dilemma this has created for national governments that want to protect domestic producers at the same time as sourcing the cheapest sugar possible. Chapter 4 turns to the labour process and the methods of exploitation used in different sugar industries, which both shape and are shaped by the industry's relative competitiveness. Chapter 5 considers the complementary processes of land exploitation, and in particular the way that industrial capital has organized the production of sugar such that it resembles 'factories in the fields'. It is here that the environmental problems linked to sugar production are also discussed, among them pollution of the soil, water and air.

Each of these chapters details the socio-ecological problems caused by the intensifying circulation of the sugar commodity (and other sucrose-based products). But by the same token, they also highlight the responses of people reforming, resisting or rejecting this process in some way. In the book's conclusion, chapter 6, these actions are joined together with other policies and practices already in existence to suggest how 'reform from below' could make sugar provisioning more ecologically sound and socially just.

CHAPTER TWO

# Growing Markets, Growing Waistlines

Too many people are eating too much sugar. That was the contention of the World Health Organization (WHO) which in 2014 proposed that the consumption of sugars – including sweeteners manufactured from corn, and natural sugars found in fruit and honey – be reduced to 5 per cent of total daily energy intake, or around 100 calories per day for an adult. For countries including the United Kingdom and United States, this would entail *more than halving* current levels of consumption, completely changing their dietary landscapes. No more bottomless refills of soft drinks, no more chocolate bars between meals and definitely one lump of sugar, not two, in the morning cup of tea!

Before we consider why the World Health Organization and other agencies working in the fields of health and nutrition have made such proposals, it is worth reflecting first on how diets in certain parts of the world became so sweet. Although there is strong evidence to suggest that humans have an innate preference for sweetness in foods, there is no physiological requirement to eat sugar in its processed form as sucrose, and certainly not in the quantities currently ingested. Yet, as Figure 2.1 suggests, at a worldwide level, the amount of sugar and other calorific sweeteners in the food system continues to grow, providing on a per capita basis more than double the amount that the WHO proposed we should actually be eating. The chapter argues that

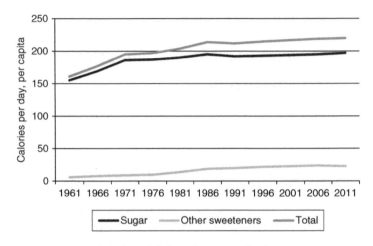

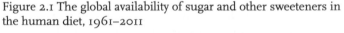

Figure 2.1 The global availability of sugar and other sweeteners in the human diet, 1961–2011

*Source*: FAOSTAT

this prevalence is due to sugar's ability to dissolve barriers to accumulation. Its chemical properties have helped food manufacturers and retailers overcome those barriers that might otherwise have restricted their sales: feelings of satiety can be suspended, eating outside of mealtimes encouraged and the taste of foods rewired without them being rejected. Sugar-sweetened industrial food can be sold more often, at more times and in more parts of the world. But by the same token, this is not something that is bound to happen simply because of the pursuit of profit. Levels of sugar consumption vary between and within countries, and in some cases it is actually decreasing, suggesting the importance of law and culture in shaping demand. Sugar may be an intoxicating substance, but it is not beyond societies to control it.

## Making markets for sugar

In his classic book *Sweetness and Power*, the anthropologist Sidney Mintz traced the historic emergence of the British sweet tooth. Within Britain, which by the nineteenth century had become the biggest consumer of sugar in the world, sugar was not originally seen as a foodstuff but variously as a medicine, condiment and decoration before then becoming more prominent as a preservative and sweetener. Market prices alone could not explain this transition. For one thing, while sugar did become cheaper over time, thanks to imports from the colonies and then from Europe, demand continued to grow even during periods when prices temporarily increased. Offering a sociology of consumption, Mintz drew attention to the way sugar became an accepted and *expected* part of the national diet. Key to this was the adoption of sugar by different classes.

For bourgeois families, sugar was used to conserve fruits, make jam and serve with tea, the kinds of activity that signified a particularly Victorian respectability in society. For labouring families, whose diets were both inadequate in calories and monotonous in taste, sugar found a ready place, along with other colonial produce such as rum, tobacco, coffee, cocoa and tea, as a 'drug food'. Mintz gave them this label because of the way they provided respite from reality – deadening hunger pangs, giving stimulus and calories, and offering new and exotic tastes. New rituals such as taking tea breaks at work and having pudding courses at home were soon established too, encouraged by the widening availability of sugar in manufactured foods like marmalade, treacle and chocolate. Indeed, consumption of sugar by the poor increased so much that by 1850 it had outgrown that of the wealthy. Sugar had gone from a rarity to ubiquity in less than a century.

Looking into the household tells us even more about this process, particularly its gendered dynamics. As the main purchasers and providers of food, it was the decisions of women which were particularly influential in the sweetening of the British diet. Female-authored cookery books were formidable advocates of sugar, proposing its increased use in breads, cakes and even salads. Others instructed women on how to be good housewives and domestic servants, providing detail on how to manipulate sugar in their own kitchens to create a variety of syrups, caramels and candies. Meanwhile, for those women who were working in factories but were still expected to manage the family's meals, sugar-sweetened foods offered the advantage of being quick and easy to prepare. It was also women and children who tended to eat disproportionately more sugar, with men consuming a larger proportion of available meat. Yet, far from enriching the female diet, sugar contributed to its simplification as combinations like jam on white bread became accepted as meals in their own right. Indeed, Mintz concluded that this maldistribution of food within the family and the subsequent undernourishment of children, especially girls, could even be described as culturally legitimized population control.

The rapid change in the type and levels of sugar consumption experienced in Britain has since been repeated in other countries. This has formed part of a worldwide 'nutrition transition' in which huge numbers of people switch to energy-dense foods. In particular, there have been marked increases in the contribution of calories from livestock, vegetable oils and sugar and other sweeteners, rendering a radical change in both the quantity and quality of national food intake. Take the case of China, in which the daily availability of sugar and sweeteners increased from 60 calories per capita in 2000 to 71 calories in 2011.[1] This equates to an extra 1 kg. bag of sugar for every man, woman and child each year and has contributed significantly to the overall increase in calorific consumption in the country. But, as Mintz cautioned, such averages tell us very little about how sugar is being eaten, by whom, and with what consequences. For this, we need to begin by looking a little closer at the way sugar has been integrated into the industrialized food system in the twentieth century.

*Sugar in the industrial food system*
Industrial foods are those that have been conceived and created not in the kitchen, but in the laboratory and factory. Produced on a scale unimaginable by the household cook or restaurant chef, they have provided convenience and cultural association for generations of largely urbanized consumers. The consumer revolution in industrial foods was spearheaded in the United States and bore a strong legacy from the Second World War. The preference given by the government to commercial, rather than home, users in sugar rations, and the lobbying of the military by companies like Hershey's and Coca-Cola to equip soldiers with chocolate and sugared drinks on account of their calorific and morale-boosting value both helped to encourage the sweetening of industrial foods. Allied to this was the increased reliance on industrial foods to save time in meal preparation. Key here was the changing role of American women, who were drawn into the factories during the war and the service sector afterwards, and who sought a way of reducing the housework burden with which they were still saddled. Food manufacturers pressed this to their advantage and sought to provide a commercial fix to a social problem.

Instant dishes had already been developed to replace time-consuming ones, like swapping steamed puddings for gelatine desserts, but soon the impetus for innovation came not from the harried housewife but from the calculating corporate manager. As documented by Michael Moss, by 1965 the Chief Executive of General Foods was making sure that the tail wagged the dog: 'Today, consumer expectations are so high and the pace at which new products are introduced is so fast that Mrs Homemaker usually can't say what it is she really wants – until after some enterprising company creates it and she finds it in a retail store.'[2] As Moss goes on to note, part of this pact with 'Mrs Homemaker' had been secured through the takeover of home economics taught in the country's schools. In 1965 when this speech was made, the American Home Economics Association had around 50,000 members. These were teaching (largely female) students how to shop around for basic ingredients and then prepare and cook them. In so doing, this cadre of professionals acted as a bulwark against the commodification of food provisioning. To rectify this, the major food manufacturers invented characters like 'Betty Crocker', a fictional mother-figure who told families it was morally acceptable to outsource food work to the factory. They also began to send out their own 'teachers' to conduct public cookery classes and flooded the Home Economics Association with funding, which perhaps explains the appointment of a General Mills executive as its president in 1987. The point here is that there was more to marketing industrial food than simply pushing a product. There was a very purposeful intent to remake social norms about what it meant to be a good wife or mother, and which continues nowadays in other guises (the good parent buying food from supermarkets because they offer vouchers for school equipment, for example). Industrial foods have to be made socially acceptable.

Product lines in soft drinks, cakes, biscuits, ice creams,

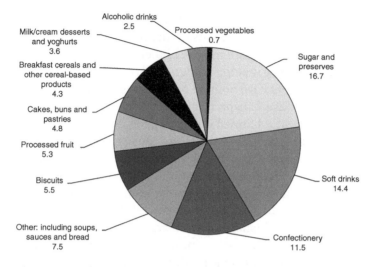

Figure 2.2 Daily grams of dietary sugars in the UK diet, 2012

*Note*: 'Sugars' refers to non-milk extrinsic sugars, which are those added to a food or released from the cell structure through processing, e.g. in fruit juice.

*Source*: Department for Environment, Food and Rural Affairs (2012) *Family Food 2012*, London: DEFRA, pp. 18–21.

desserts, chocolates, sweets and many more have all since grown in volume and range, marked out by their qualities of durability, accessibility and affordability. Certainly in advanced capitalist economies, they have become the primary vehicles of sugar provisioning: the majority of sugar is now sold for use in the food and drink manufacturing industry, rather than for direct consumption for use as table sugar or in home-cooked recipes. This has effectively corporatized the control of sugar content. Food survey data from the United Kingdom provides evidence of this evolution. It shows an average daily intake of 77 grams of added sugar – equivalent to 312 calories, far above dietary guidelines – most of which is consumed indirectly, 'hidden' as it were. In fact, because food survey participants tend to under-report food eaten outside the home and in between meals, the actual figure may be higher still.[3]

The idea of sugar being hidden is worth exploring further. Many observers have pointed out that sugar is not just contained in the 'usual suspects' of sweet treats, but in things like pizzas, sauces and tinned vegetables, too. Sugar has become a favoured ingredient of the food industry not just because of the sweetness it imparts. In some cartons of orange juice, for example, alongside the natural sugars of the squeezed oranges, liquid invert sugar can be found. This provides a sweeter taste but also has more powerful preserving qualities than normal table sugar, meaning that consumers are treated to an instant taste sensation and retailers to longer periods in which to sell the product (freshly squeezed orange juice will only last a few days before it starts to go off). In its own small way, this modification of orange juice is nothing less than the defiance of the temporality of nature itself.

This mastery of time that sugar helped to facilitate was aided by further developments in canning, freezing, refrigeration and dehydration, which also sought to override the natural perishability of food. Products like tinned pineapple, chilled desserts and condensed milk would thus become readily available, again supported by cookbooks, which this time educated housewives on how to store, prepare and serve the sugar-containing products that would stock their new domestic appliances such as fridge-freezers.

The movement of industrial foods around the world was thus made easier by their durability, but was really expedited by the liberalization of trade and investment rules. This allowed companies to export processed food directly or manufacture them in target markets using cheap imported ingredients. For example, in Central America, as average tariffs declined from 45 per cent to 6 per cent between 1985 and 2000, the level of food imports doubled, most of which came from the United States.[4]

Added to this have been changes in the places in which food is bought, such as the replacement of fresh or 'wet' markets by supermarkets. In Latin America, for example, the supermarkets' share of all retail food sales increased from 15 per cent in 1990 to 60 per cent by 2000.[5] Supermarkets have encouraged the consumption of sugar not only by stocking wide ranges of industrial foods but also by enabling bulk-buying and impulse-buying, often through promotional discounts which can lead to unintended (over)consumption. Like fast-food restaurants, cinemas and shopping malls, they have also provided the cultural space in which customers can understand and appreciate new, often western-origin, products.

Other traders of industrial foods are smaller in scale than the retail giants but no less influential in establishing the commercial and cultural conduits along which sugar travels. The installation of refrigerators and freezers in convenience stores, often encouraged by soft drinks and ice cream companies whose brands are then emblazoned upon them, allows cooling beverages and snacks to be sold, readily appreciated in hotter parts of the world. Other retailers, such as petrol stations, have *become* convenience stores. Like the fast-food restaurant, they evince a ready fit between sweetened foods and life on the road.

In those areas lacking fixed retail infrastructure, typically home to poorer and more remote communities, petty traders or higglers, such as the thousands of women contracted by Nestlé in Brazil, sell bite-size snacks targeted at those with only a little spare cash. Finally, the vending machine, perhaps the apotheosis of the industrial retail system, offers food from nowhere, sold by no one, 24/7. There are an estimated 18 million of these automated

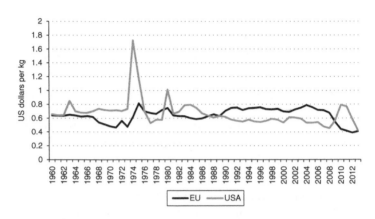

Figure 2.3 Real price of raw sugar in the EU and the United States, 1960–2013

*Source*: World Bank Global Economic Monitor Commodities. Prices are in constant 2000 US$

'micro-distributors' worldwide, many ironically secreted in sites associated with healthy lifestyles such as leisure centres, parks and hospitals – a perfect example of the contradictory imperative to live well and eat poorly.[6]

But this is not just a story of durable manufacturing and accessible retailing. The pervasiveness of sugar in the contemporary foodscape is also intimately related to the industrialization of agriculture, which has kept sugar affordable as a raw material. As shown in Figure 2.3, the real price of sugar in the European Union (EU) and the United States, adjusted for inflation, has rarely strayed above 80 cents a kilogram (in 2000 prices) throughout the last five decades. In other words, even in national markets in which sugar has been heavily protected and traditionally kept above world market prices, food manufacturers have had consistent access to large volumes of sugar that have been fairly stable in price.

The importance of cheap sugar to food manufacturers can be illustrated by another graph (Figure 2.4), this time showing the cost of sugar as a proportion of a product's retail price. These are all products high in sugar content: apart from water, sugar was one of the top three ingredients in every one. Moreover, all of the products were on special offer, positioned in prime places in the supermarket, such as at the end of an aisle, and given an average price reduction of one-third. Both these things suggest that sugar should account for a significant proportion of their final selling price, but, as shown in the graph, it was typically between 2 and 12 per cent. The four-pack of Red Bull for example – which contains nothing but water, sugar and some taurine, caffeine and vitamin additives – sold at a retail price of £3.00, yet included just £0.06 worth of sugar.

This suggests that sugar-sweetened products offer manufacturers large margins to play with, to be soaked up by transport costs, marketing budgets, slotting fees to retailers, and pay-outs to their managers and shareholders.[7] To this end it is perhaps no surprise that many of the brands shown in the graph have all been acquired by multinational food conglomerates in recent years, including Ski by Nestlé, Ben & Jerry's by Unilever, McVitie's by Turkish-based Yildiz Holding and Hartley's jam by US-based Hain Celestial Group. For proponents of health taxes, it also strengthens the case for taxing the product rather than sugar itself since any likely increase in the cost of this ingredient would make little difference in the final product price.

The industrialization of agriculture also refers to the standardization of sugar quality and its fractioning into various ingredients, providing the kind of inputs that mass manufacturers require. In the nineteenth century, the development of vacuum pan and centrifugal technology

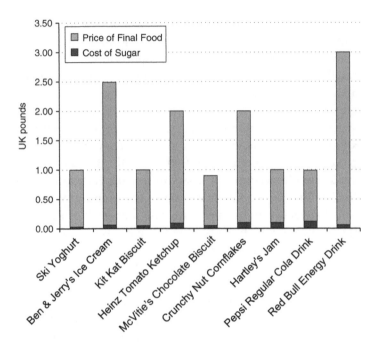

Figure 2.4 Cost of sugar in final foods, 2014

*Note*: Data collected during in-store visit by the author to the Leamington Spa branch of Tesco's supermarket in December 2014. Cost of sugar based on the annual average EU white sugar price between August 2013 and August 2014 and multiplied by grams of sugar content calculated from product's nutritional label.

allowed for greater control over the evaporation of sugar juice and the separation of sucrose crystals from molasses, resulting in higher sugar retention and functionally differentiated products. These came to include granular table sugar, fine castor sugar and powdered icing sugar (all white sugars); light/dark sugar, muscovado sugar and demerara sugar (all brown sugars); dissolved sugar and invert sugar (both liquid sugars); and a range of syrups and molasses. Ultimately, each of these provided its own set of attributes in the preparation, preservation, presentation and eating process – from a glossy finish to a textured 'mouthfeel'.

In comparison, more artisanal forms of sugar production were less amenable to the factory food system. These jaggery sugars are made by boiling cane juice in an open pan and draining the molasses using gravity. They can be found across the world and are usually known by their colloquial names: *gur* in India, *panela* in Latin America, *wasanbon* in Japan. Although they are still consumed today, they do not offer the value, volume, versatility and above all *predictability* of industrial sugars. Instead, these artefacts of pre-capitalist production have been pushed to the margins of the modern food system.[8]

The reduction of agricultural products to industrial inputs has been dubbed 'substitutionism' by the rural sociologists David Goodman, Bernando Sorj and John Wilkinson. What they mean by this is that foodstuffs are made into readily interchangeable commodities whose usage is then determined solely by cost and technical criteria. In other words, if a manufacturer can save money by substituting one ingredient for another without damaging the appeal of the final food, then they will.

In the case of sugar, there have been three distinct moments of substitutionism. The first was the production of sucrose from sugar beet rather than cane, which produced a chemically identical substance that in nineteenth-century Europe would replace much of the sugar previously imported from the Americas and the East Indies.

The second was the invention of corn and wheat syrups, made by wet-milling the starchy crops and then using enzymes to change some of the glucose into fructose to provide sweetness, hence the name *high* fructose corn syrup. This was developed in the United States in the 1970s, offering corn refiners a way to dispose of the surpluses of the grain regime at a time when the already inflated price of sugar was pushed higher by deregulation. HFCS also took off in Japan and South Korea, which, again, used American corn as the feedstock, imported duty-free as part of their post-war integration into the US-centred grain regime.

The third moment of sucrose substitution was the invention of artificial sweeteners, a category of ingredients now worth US$2 billion globally. These include saccharin (sold under brand names such as 'Sweet 'n Low'), aspartame (NutraSweet) and sucralose (Splenda). Although these additives are non-calorific, like HFCS they had the same effect of moving the production of sweetness away from biological processes occurring in the field and towards chemical manipulation managed in the factory.

These attempts to squeeze biological uncertainty out of production by reducing dependence on capricious natural processes have led food manufacturers to build closer links with chemical and pharmaceutical firms. For their part, primary processing firms have turned into suppliers of generic food ingredients – proteins, carbohydrates, fats, flavours and sugars – around which final foods can be designed. A good example here is Tate & Lyle, which in 2010 sold its long-standing sugar-refining business to concentrate on what it calls 'speciality food ingredients and solutions'. Among the ingredients it now sells are Splenda®, PrOatein™ and a stevia-based sweetener called TASTEVA®.

One outcome of the constant search for cheaper, functionally differentiated and nutritionally enhanced ingredients, then, has been to weaken the historic links between food and crop. The proliferation of foods claiming to be sugar-free, 'lite' and low-calorie is one manifestation of this. Another is the combination of sucrose and non-sucrose sugars performing a variety of tasks. Take the Nutri-Grain cereal bar made by Kellogg's. Among other things, this contains corn syrup, HFCS, sugar, glycerin, maltodextrol, honey, dextrose and sorbitol – an edible division of labour you might say!

Although this process of substitutionism might seem quite technical, it has in fact been highly politicized. Depending on the threat posed, various coalitions of companies have formed to try and keep potential competitors out of their markets. Barriers to entry have been constructed through a variety of state-sanctioned measures. In the EU, for example, sugar-beet and sugar-cane producers have benefited from the border tariffs and tiny production quotas that kept a lid on HFCS sales.

Other policy instruments that have been invoked include regulatory approval, patent protection, dietary guidelines and restrictions on labelling claims. For example, in 2008 in the United States, the Sugar Association attempted to get the Food and Drug Administration to redefine the label 'natural' to distinguish between sugar and HFCS, because 'natural' should refer only to products containing nothing artificial, synthetic or more than minimally processed. They said that HFCS fell outside this category as its production requires changing the molecular structure in a naturally found product, whereas, when sugar is refined, this molecular structure is merely extracted. Replying in kind, the Corn Refiners Association countered that HFCS is natural because it uses enzymes rather than inorganic chemicals to transform the glucose into fructose. Whilst demurring on an actual definition, the Food and Drug Administration sided with the sugar producers by suggesting that suppliers of HFCS avoid making 'all natural ingredients' claims in the future.

Attempts to defend market sales through institutionalized forms of exclusion are nothing new. An investigation by Gary Taubes and Cristin Kearns Couzens turned up evidence which showed that in the 1960s the US sugar industry spent millions of dollars in today's money to study every conceivable harmful effect of the artificial sweetener cyclamate.[9] Eventually, one study linked it to bladder cancer in rats, leading the Food and Drug Administration to ban the additive, although later research showed this link not to be relevant to humans.

As well as legal interventions acting as a bulwark against substitutionism, the complete interchangeability of ingredients also remains hampered by their physical properties. The social scientists Ben Fine, Michael Heasman and Judith Wright have noted that sweetened corn syrups have been restricted largely to the soft drinks market because they are produced in liquid form and are not appropriate for other products[10]; likewise, because artificial sweeteners can be up to 2,000 times as sweet as sugar, they are only added in small quantities and therefore cannot add bulk to foods. Indeed, for these authors, artificial sweeteners are seen more as supplements than substitutes for sugar, slotting into discrete markets for 'diet' drinks and 'low calorie' foods, and expanding the market for sweetness as a whole. This is particularly important for the argument that the adverse health effects of sugary foods can be avoided through product reformulation since it suggests that such products will simply be offered alongside, and consumed in addition to, existing 'full sugar' products.

Taken together, the legal and sensory limits to substitutionism, along with certain price advantages, have meant that predictions about the 'end of sugar' have failed to come to fruition. Despite the manufacture of test-tube sweeteners like aspartame, we have seen in the global expansion of sugar cane and beet the consolidation of plant-based sweetening systems.

But there is also another reason why sugar cane and sugar beet remain important parts of world agriculture: substitutionism cuts both ways. Sugar processors are not just in the business of making sucrose and have sought to make fuller use of their cane/beet throughput. Molasses, a viscous by-product of sugar processing, has been sold as a foodstuff, an animal feed, a feedstock for rum and now biofuel. Since most of the cane and beet plant is not actually sugar, there is also lots of biomass left over. Bagasse, the dried cane pulp remaining after the sugar juice has been extracted, has been used to produce heat, electricity, paper, plastics and chemicals. As some of these other revenue streams become more secure, as has happened with ethanol biofuel, sugar processors have shifted from one output to the other, reducing their dependence on specific agro-food chains. As outlined in the previous chapter, the dynamics of farming cannot be determined solely by reference to what people are eating.

## Unpacking the nutrition transition

Let us return to the notion of an international nutrition transition. We previously discussed the spread of industrial foods in the United Kingdom and the United States but these two countries are no longer where the frontiers of accumulation lie. By way of example, Coca-Cola's sales between 2008 and 2013 grew between 5 and 7 per cent in their regional divisions of Africa, the Middle East, Russia, South and East Asia, and Latin America. In contrast, the number of bottles sold in North America and Europe barely budged.[11] In this respect, Coca-Cola, the world's biggest single user of sugar, is representative of the food industry as a whole.[12] Data shows that, across the same period, per capita sugar consumption was growing most quickly in

Malaysia, Venezuela, Bolivia, Sudan and South Africa, whilst remaining stagnant in North America and even declining in Europe.[13] So what accounts for these dietary transformations and the great shifting of sweetness to the Global South?

Economic analyses have pointed towards market incentives, focusing not so much on the falling price of foods but on the rising purchasing power of a 'global middle class'. At lower levels of income, sweetened foods are believed to have a higher elasticity of demand. This means that poor people who suddenly have a little more money in their pocket are more likely to spend it on extra sugar consumption than those at higher levels of income who have already sated their demand. There is an intuitive appeal to this argument and a number of studies have found strong correlation between changes in per capita income and corresponding levels of sugar consumption.[14] But correlation is not causation and, taking our cue from Mintz again, it is important to socialize the experience of capitalist development if we are to understand why this seems to result in people eating more sugar.

For instance, as certain groups become more affluent, they are likely to be targeted by the food industry as potential customers. Already, huge amounts of money are spent promoting sweetened foods. The nutritionist-cum-sociologist Marion Nestle has the total expenditure by the food industry on direct media advertising in the United States at US$11 billion, with nearly 70 per cent of this for convenience foods, snacks and candies, desserts and alcoholic and soft drinks. The marketing techniques honed here have been duplicated in developing countries. A multi-country study in South and East Asia by Consumers International found that around half of the television adverts screened to children were for food products, mostly those of little nutritive value, and that the majority of children believed these were also fit for frequent consumption.[15]

There is another aspect of marketing to children, which is their very constitution as consumers. It is commonly accepted that, by virtue of eating, every individual is also a food consumer. However, this conflates two meanings of the word 'consume': one to ingest, the other to buy. So while children certainly ingest food, they tend not to acquire that food themselves through market purchases. Thus the real success of advertising to children has not simply been to make them desire certain products with increasing regularity, but to actualize them as consumers with influence over the household budget. The resulting 'pester power' accorded to even very young children not only encourages the steady introduction of foods high in fat, salt and sugar into their diets as they begin to shape household expenditure, it also stimulates nagging and negotiation with their carers – a family challenge that again tends to fall on women's shoulders.

For older children in more commercialized societies, carers may have even less control over dietary patterns and shopping habits. The psychologist Sandra Calvert has argued that, due to the increased levels of discretionary income (e.g. pocket money) acquired by children in the United States, and the existence of child-specific TV stations and websites, food manufacturers wield more influence than ever before. Children now view approximately 40,000 advertisements each year, with those under 8 years of age lacking the cognitive development to even understand their function as adverts.[16] Again, these trends are emerging in poorer countries too. Writing in 2000, the anthropologist Guo Yuhua noted how the 'little emperors' in China have acquired a marketing-mediated knowledge of food and use pocket money from their parents and grandparents to acquire these typically forbidden treats. In fact, the very term 'children's food' is relatively new in the country, these being marked out from 'adult foods' by their association with fun and novelty, rather than nutrition and tradition.[17]

Nor have adults been spared the appeals of the multinationals. As discussed in the previous section, an intrinsic part of marketing is about tapping into social desires, suggesting how they could be fulfilled through consumption. In the Chinese chocolate market, for example, efforts have been made to teach people about what constitutes good-quality, aspirational chocolate. Exhibitions, such as the *Salon de Chocolat* hosted in Beijing featuring, among other things, models draped in confectionery, have been established to inform cultural entrepreneurs that certain products – in this case luxury chocolates made by European companies – are part of what it means to spend well and live a cultured life.

Not all campaigns are so lavish, and, depending on the market segment being targeted, different strategies will be adopted. A meal out at McDonald's might be presented as a way to register the upward mobility of a family, a bottle of Coca-Cola as a communion with the modern world. In his own words, the president of Coca-Cola, Muhtar Kent, once described the drink as 'an idea, a vision, a feeling'.[18] Rather grandiose terms for a mixture of water, sweetener and colourings, but not without basis. The point here is that the demand for sweet industrial foods is not naturally emerging but actively brought into being by the efforts of the food industry.

There are also broader societal changes at work, tied up with the development of global capitalism, which have expedited the spread of sugar. The entry of women into the workforce as part of the proletarianization of peasantries across the Global South has been of huge importance. Despite their additional work outside the home, women still bear social obligations to feed the family, meaning that many have turned to pre-prepared foods to help manage the 'double burden'. The disjunctures brought by rapid industrialization, such as migration to hectic urban areas and flexible and precarious working patterns, have also meant that eating is less regulated by the steady rhythms of mealtimes, leading to a rise in snacking. Finally, as part of capitalism's thrust to colonize ever more areas of social life, sweetened foods such as ready meals, packed-lunch items and infant formula have been created to replace non-market forms of cooking and breastfeeding, while cultural celebrations like birthdays and religious events are targeted as commercial opportunities to sell sweetened foods as gifts. Via each of these three processes, the very environment in which food provisioning takes place is transformed, meaning that the changes in sugar consumption experienced alongside economic growth cannot be put down to extra disposable income alone.

The account presented so far suggests a uniform transformation of diets and the seeming global supremacy of sugar. However, things are more complex than this as evidenced in these two empirical observations. The first is the fact that there are significant variations at the national level between average income and average sugar consumption. This is detailed in Figure 2.5. The four biggest consumers of sugar and sweeteners on the right-hand side of the graph, at least according to data on sugar availability, are the United States, Switzerland, Trinidad and Tobago, and Cuba – countries with very different levels of GDP per capita. Equally, some countries that are relatively wealthy, such as Japan, Spain and Slovenia, have much less sugar and sweetener in their diet. What this illustrates is the fact

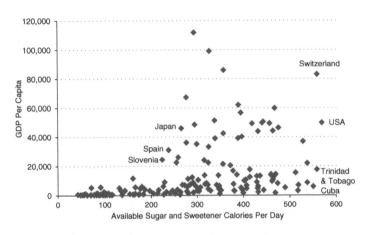

Figure 2.5 International comparison of sugar and sweetener consumption, 2014

*Source*: World Bank and FAOSTAT.

that food culture and economic history remain important in shaping to what extent a nutrition transition is experienced in relation to sugar.

One consequence of this for multinational companies is that they may have to adapt their marketing strategies. There are many examples of failed launches and unexpected turns. Kellogg's abandoned its plan to sell cereals in Asia because they did not fit with the low-milk style of Asian breakfasting, leaving the company to focus on dry cereal bars instead. Likewise, in China, sugar consumption has long been supressed vis-à-vis western countries because tea is not drunk with sugar. More recently, as traditional herbal teas have undergone their own industrialization process, now sold under brand names in cans and cartons, they have come to challenge the supremacy of sweetened soft drinks. In 2006, one of these Chinese brands, Wanglaoji, replaced Coca-Cola as the number-one soft drink by volume sales, prompting the latter to launch its own ready-to-drink green tea with herbal ingredients.

Not only are socially embedded diets difficult to remake or override, in some cases, governments or political groups might actively defend food cultures against these multinational 'industrial interlopers'. Campaigns to promote traditional dishes in South Korea or protest against fast-food restaurants in the Middle East spring to mind here as another set of barriers preventing the total embrace of sugar-laden diets.

The second empirical observation is that in some societies, especially in the Global North, sugar consumption is actually *decreasing*. In the United Kingdom, for example, average per capita intake is thought to have peaked in the 1950s. More recent and accurate data confirms a downward trend, reporting decreasing consumption in the country between 2007 and 2012, with some but not all of that change explained by rising prices for food.[19]

Building on this point, many epidemiologists no longer talk about a single nutrition transition from 'traditional' starchy diets to 'modern' energy-dense diets. Barry Popkin, a renowned chronicler of dietary change, has proposed another nutrition transition in which behavioural change begins to undermine the tendencies towards excessive meat, sugar and oil consumption and people begin instead to eat higher-quality fats, less refined carbohydrates and more whole grains, fruits and vegetables.[20] However, in the UK case, as we noted earlier, the total amount of sugar consumed still exceeds government recommendations, suggesting that a national-level transition to a low-sugar diet still has some way to go.

The implications of this argument are twofold. First, it reinforces the importance of studying populations based on categories other than nationality since consumption remains marked by race, class and gender too. In the United Kingdom, it is the poorest in society that eat more sugary food than the richest; in the United States, black Americans are much more likely than white Americans to receive an excessive amount of the daily calorific intake from sugar.[21] These differences have not occurred by chance. Studies from the United States have concluded that Afro-Americans and Hispanic Americans have been targeted with more marketing for high-calorie foods and beverages than white Americans.[22] In short, those groups 'graduating' to healthier diets tend to be those already advantaged in society. Moreover, those individuals unable to escape the lure of industrial food face problems beyond poor health. Due to size discrimination, some people – especially women – who have become obese have found it harder to gain employment and earn the same wages as the rest of their cohort, in effect being punished twice over.[23]

The second implication is that we need to identify the factors which explain the turn away from sugar consumption. Chief among these is the attack upon sugar by medical professionals.

*Health advocacy*
As noted earlier, for much of its history sugar was actually treated as a medicine, cited as a cure for stomach ills and fevers across the Islamic and Christian worlds. Sidney Mintz even noted how the phrase 'an apothecary without sugar' came to mean a state of utter desolation or helplessness. The balance of expert opinion has since shifted, of course, and now it is the adverse health effects of sugar that are the focus of physicians and medical researchers.

The most heated debates have taken place around the link between sugar and non-communicable diseases, including diabetes, cardiovascular diseases and cancers. The stakes of this debate could not be higher. Non-communicable diseases are the leading cause of mortality in the world, killing 36 million people in 2008, mostly in poorer countries, it should be added. Unhealthy diets are said to be one of the key contributors to the four major risk factors of these diseases, which are increases in blood pressure, in blood glucose, cholesterol and body fat.[24] Yet if restrictions are placed upon the consumption of products deemed unhealthy, businesses could lose billions, with no guarantee – some have argued – that the premature death of millions will be avoided.

The concerns about sugar can be split into two broad camps. The first posits sugar consumption as having an indirect effect on health in so far as it leads to unhealthy diets and various forms of malnutrition. This is related to the notion of the 'empty calorie'. Devised with the advent of nutritional science, this phrase communicated the idea that, while sugar and other sweeteners like HFCS provide energy, unlike other naturally sugary foods like fruit they do not contain any other nutrients. Whereas in previous centuries the purity and whiteness of sugar was something to venerate, now these qualities are cast as something altogether more sinister – and with good reason.

For example, in Mumbai, the Indian government has reported that 25 per cent of children aged 0–6 years suffer from high levels of acute malnutrition. What is surprising is that this is not down to a lack of food nor to absolute poverty, but to the reliance of children on a diet of 'fun-size' sweet and salty snacks purchased from roadside vendors.[25] Dependence on empty calories is particularly worrying in this context. While adults can recover from acute malnutrition, in young children it has long-term consequences, among them inhibiting their physiological and mental development.

Alongside this, it has also been argued that sweetened products tend not to sate the appetite and so are eaten in addition to usual consumption patterns. Thus, empty calories are said to displace more nutritious foods from the diet and/or add excessive calories to it. This can produce under-nutrition (a lack of micronutrients) and over-nutrition (an excess of calories) side by side.

Supporting this account, and revisiting our earlier discussion of sugar as a 'drug food', recent neurological research has proposed that sugary foods are eaten to excess because they are genuinely addictive. The claim is that when sugar is eaten in equal proportion to fat, dopamine is released in the brain which overrides the regulatory functions that tell us we are full. So foods like doughnuts and ice cream, as well as sugary and fatty foods designed to be eaten simultaneously – the burger, fries and soft drink, for example – have 'hedonic' effects which actually make it difficult to stop consuming. Weight gain and eating disorders like bingeing might therefore be seen in the same light as bodily and behavioural change linked to alcohol or cocaine abuse.

The second concern about sugar consumption is its direct effects on health as an independent risk factor for disease. In other words, sugar is toxic and too much can make you ill. Two polemical books have been of particular political importance in this debate. In his 1972 book *Pure, White and Deadly* – note the drug metaphor again – the physiologist John Yudkin proposed that sugar and not fat was to blame for the growing incidence of heart disease.[26] Yudkin's ideas caused a storm of controversy, not least because of the way they were explicitly presented as a critique of corporate manipulation of the general public. He was vilified by the industry and many of his ideas, including links between sugar and diabetes, were exiled from the public imagination.

However, they have since been revived by the clinical paediatrician Robert Lustig, who in his 2012 book *Fat Chance*[27] claimed to have found the causal pathway by which sugar directly harms the body and which had unfortunately eluded Yudkin. In brief, Lustig argued that it was sugar's effect on insulin levels and the metabolism that was crucial. Sugar, and specifically the fructose component of sucrose, is metabolized primarily in the liver, whereas glucose contained in starchy carbohydrates is metabolized in cells around the body. If too much fructose is consumed too quickly, the liver has to convert much of it to fat, ultimately inducing insulin resistance and an inability of the body to regulate the way calories are stored. This in turn triggers the processes that lead to diabetes, heart disease and obesity. Thus, for Lustig and other proponents of this idea, the important thing is not necessarily to reduce total calorie intake but to reduce concentrated fructose intake, regulating the consumption of sucrose-covered cereals, HFCS-sweetened drinks and processed fruit juices among others.

What is the status of these twin concerns in the broader scientific literature? Reviewing the body of controlled trials and cohort studies conducted into sugar consumption and obesity, the academic nutritionist Jim Mann found consistent evidence that increasing or decreasing intake of dietary sugars did have a small but meaningful effect on body weight.[28] Similarly, a study by the epidemiologist Sanjay Basu based on population data concluded that the intake of sugars appeared to have a direct link to diabetes, aside from its effects via obesity.[29]

Others have remained more circumspect. Responding to

Lustig's claims, the British Nutrition Foundation reported that major scientific reviews did not find sufficient evidence to prove that total sugar intake causes obesity or diabetes, although consumption of sugar-sweetened beverages specifically was recognized as a potential problem. In sum, while the close correlation between different forms of sugar consumption and the incidence of obesity, diabetes and other life-threatening illnesses is widely noted, the balance of evidence has not yet shifted to the point where a causal role for sugar is accepted as the scientific common sense. Sugar is not yet being treated as the new tobacco.

The comparison with tobacco has often been made by health campaigners for obvious reasons. Not only does it draw parallels between the accumulative long-term effects of eating sugary foods and smoking cigarettes, but it also tars opponents of anti-sugar campaigns with the brush of corporate conspiracy. There have certainly been enough reports about the nefarious activities of the sugar industry to infer that, just like the tobacco industry, they are deliberately obfuscating research that threatens their bottom line.

An investigation by Garry Taubes and Cristin Kearns Couzens detailed how the Sugar Association in the United States spent hundreds of thousands of dollars in the 1970s on studies purposely designed to obscure the findings of other scientists evaluating the effects of sugar.[30] Such 'pollution' of the scientific environment continues today. For example, Taubes and Kearns Couzens went on to report that the authors of the 2010 United States Department of Agriculture (USDA) dietary guidelines cited two scientific reviews as evidence that sugary drinks do not make adults fat: one written by a nutrition consultant whose clients included the World Sugar Research Organisation, the other by the former research manager of the United Kingdom's Sugar Bureau.

Nor are these apparent conflicts of interest confined to the health effects of sucrose. The journalist Felicity Lawrence has written of the controversy that accompanied a 2006 review by the European Food Safety Authority into links between aspartame and cancer. The review involved scientists who had their impartiality questioned because they had either been employed by or received funding from aspartame manufacturers and companies that used this sweetener.[31]

As well as working closely with medical professionals by sponsoring academic journals, conferences and research studies, the food industry has engaged in a variety of lobbying activities. Marion Nestle has highlighted the successful effort by various companies dealing in sugar to change the wording of the USDA dietary guidelines from 'choose food and beverages *that limit* your intake of sugars' to 'choose food and beverages *to moderate* your intake of sugars'.[32] Their influence in this case was assured through a combination of financial contributions to political parties and individual politicians, as well as personal contacts established in key state agencies by virtue of their 'revolving door' recruitment practices. In another example, also from the United States, the Sugar Association lobbied elected politicians in Congress to withdraw its annual US$406 million funding of the World Health Organization in response to the latter's 2003 report which advised that sugar consumption be reduced to 10 per cent of daily calorific intake.

All things considered, it is easy to see how nutrition science and state regulation can become deeply compromised by the political activities of the food industry (indeed, a chapter of Nestle's book is called 'Politics versus Science'). But without apologizing for the activities of the so-called 'sugar lobby', it is important to recognize the limits of this analysis. In essence, what this does is to blame current outcomes on the obfuscation of 'genuine' science by the corrupting influence of food politics. What it therefore overlooks is the importance of culinary practices, food prices, shopping patterns and other social factors in shaping sugar consumption.

First, it is worth remembering that a widely accepted causal link between sugar consumption and a major non-communicable disease already exists: that of dental caries or tooth decay. This is the most common chronic disease in childhood and results in pain, functional impairment and social handicap for millions. Still in the United Kingdom, more than 500 children aged five to nine are admitted to hospital *every week* because of rotten teeth, although, like other diseases that have accompanied the nutrition transition, dental decay is now more of a burden in regions beyond Western Europe and North America.[33]

As to its cause, even the industry-funded World Sugar Research Organisation has not denied that the frequency of sugar consumption is inextricably linked to the spread of acid plaque in the mouth. Yet, despite this recognition, there hardly seems to have been an international overhaul of adolescent eating habits worthy of the problem. Like the appeal for overweight people to do more exercise, oral health campaigns have promoted better self-management, or more precisely better parenting, through regular brushing with fluoride toothpaste – a way to override excessive sugar consumption rather than reduce it in the first place.

Second, for 'genuine' medical research to affect health outcomes, it must enter the arena of public debate and itself become politicized. This can be discerned by looking at the way appeals to the state have been made by health campaigners, monetizing the cost of treating a particular disease and warning of an impending economic crisis unless action is taken without delay. Members of the UK group Action on Sugar, for example, have argued that obesity and diabetes cost the UK taxpayer £5 billion a year and that, without regulation, this will increase tenfold by the year 2050.[34] At its most hyperbolic, reformers have even warned that 'diabesity' (Type II diabetes brought on by weight gain) will bankrupt countries around the world within decades, creating a discursive imperative to find a scapegoat like sugar that can serve as a point of intervention.[35] In this sense, rather than seeing politics as an oppositional force to authentic medical truth, as Nestle's formulation 'Politics versus Science' would have us believe, it is preferable to see politics as the means by which truth claims are made powerful, regardless of whether the person making them is connected to the sugar industry or not.

Health claims can be politicized in different ways. While most demands of the sort made by Action on Sugar are concerned with national regulation of sugar consumption, some have gone further and presented the problem as a resolutely global one. The Lancet Non-Communicable Diseases Action Group – an informal collaboration of medical academics, practitioners and civil society organizations – have dubbed the spread of diabetes and other diseases an industrial 'epidemic', an epidemic whose vectors are not biological agents but multinational corporations.[36] By focusing attention on a particular category of business, these arguments have a different political resonance, amplifying animosity towards cultural imperialism or underlining the need for international regulation, such as the proposed Global Convention for Healthy Diets modelled on the WHO Framework Convention on Tobacco Control.

But underlying all these demands, whether national or global in orientation, is the idea that sugar is not just harming individual consumers but also placing unbearable fiscal and productive strains on the 'body politic' as a whole. Indeed, the same logic applies to legal action brought by states, as opposed to individuals, against the food industry for knowingly burdening them with avoidable health costs. Asking companies to take responsibility for such negative externalities has put health campaigners on a collision course with the very imperatives of capital, a clash which has marked many attempts to change the way that sugar consumption is governed.

## Governing consumption

The opposing logics of health campaigners and capitalists was vividly highlighted in 2012 when New York City's Board of Health, publicly supported by Mayor Bloomberg, sought to introduce a ban on sugary soft drinks bigger than 16 ounces being sold in the city's restaurants and stadiums. It was a measure designed to curb obesity by limiting ingestion of 'supersize' single servings and challenging the normalization of dietary excess. Predictably, it met with fierce opposition from the food industry, which fomented public opposition by, among other things, sponsoring a promotional campaign through the 'Consumer Freedom Group' that lambasted the proposed ban as an attack on the fundamental liberties of Americans. The decision was ultimately dragged through the New York State legal system, wherein the Court of Appeals ultimately sided with the American Beverage Association and declared it an overreach of the Board of Health's legislative powers.

What this draws our attention to is the role of the state, which has hitherto been underplayed in our analysis, depicted as a passive victim of business lobbying and not much beyond. Certainly, the purveyors of industrial food have developed a familiar repertoire of tactics in such regulatory battles. These are: (a) appeal to the 'mixed messages' of scientists around the health effects of sugar and the wisdom of existing dietary guidelines; (b) defend the freedom to consume at the same time as encouraging individual restraint; and (c) displace demands for behavioural change into offsetting activities such as regular exercise and better dental hygiene. Yet this approach has not always been successful and it is worth reflecting as much, if not more, on the political defeats of the collective capitalist interest as on their victories.

Despite stiff opposition from many of the same companies that contested the New York bill the year before, in 2013 the Mexican government managed to pass legislation which levied taxes to the equivalent of 10 per cent on sweetened drinks and 8 per cent on energy-dense 'junk food'. Key to passing the bill was gaining cross-party support for a broad package of reforms – of which the 'fat tax' was just one – that raised much-needed government revenue. Electoral support was also assured by earmarking the tax for providing potable water in all the country's schools, a de-commodification of drinking that also threatened to erode the market for bottled soft drinks.

Although similar taxes have been levied in other countries, this was rightly seen as a major blow to the power of the food industry. Mexico had recently surpassed the United States as the country with the highest proportion of people deemed overweight and obese ('the fattest nation on earth' as it was dubbed in the media) and was also the highest per capita consumer of soft drinks. Beneficial effects have already been claimed for the bill. A follow-up study conducted the following year by the country's National Institute of Public Health measured the decline in sugary beverage consumption at 10 per cent during the first three months of 2014, compared with the same period the year before.[37]

And nor was it just in Mexico that the legislation had an effect. Reacting to the country's reform bill, the credit agency Moody's subsequently lowered its outlook for the global beverage industry as a whole, sending a powerful signal to investors that worldwide profits were likely to fall. Indeed, in its annual report to shareholders that same year, Coca-Cola listed obesity concerns as the number-one risk factor affecting their business. Above water scarcity, economic competition and a failure to expand its operations, it was acknowledged that the possibility of government regulation and negative publicity around obesity 'could adversely affect our profitability'.[38]

The prospect of a 'domino effect' of anti-sugar legislation has stung many in the food industry into action. This was encapsulated by Debra Sandler, the head of Mars Chocolate in North America, when she said: 'If we don't [act], I worry that someone else will do it for us . . . Don't wait for regulators to tell us what to do.'[39] The result has been a spate of self-regulation and 'voluntary' compromises enacted by business. These have included measures like reducing advertising to very young children, re-sizing portions and reformulating products. Some critics have charged that this approach is simply a way of co-opting regulators. Take the case of product reformulation. Its appeal to health advocates lies in the way it weakens the 'sugar lobby' by pitting food manufacturers against sugar producers since the former might be able to maintain rates of profit without necessarily selling as much sugar. A soft drink sweetened with aspartame might be no less profitable than one sweetened by sugar.

However, whether this 'divide and conquer' strategy actually improves dietary health in practice remains debatable.

I have already mentioned the argument that 'sugar-free' products might end up supplementing rather than substituting for their more calorific counterparts. Added to this is the danger that simply switching the source of sweetness might not necessarily make for healthier diets. Rather, low-sugar products become phantom foods, 'sweet nothings' which provide barely any nutritional content at all. According to some studies, these do not activate the body's food reward pathways in the same way as the 'full sugar' food does and so fail to provide the same level of satiety.[40] By reinforcing the normalization of sweetness, it has been argued that these low-calorie alternatives also encourage people to seek out more of the same taste, thereby ingesting sugar through some other route. The risk is that low-calorie sweeteners will be used only in nutritionally vacant and gastronomically bland foods that might actually encourage additional eating. So, as the neurobiologist Qing Yang concluded, rather than replacing sugar with its low-calorie counterparts, '*unsweetening* the world's diet may be the key to reversing the obesity epidemic'.[41]

Another aspect to the food industry's product reformulation strategy has been 'nutrification', whereby micronutrients have been added to sugary foods like breakfast cereals and toaster pastries. To give them appeal to health-conscious consumers, Kellogg's Pop Tarts have been fortified with iron and vitamins, and emblazoned on the front with the words 'Made with real fruit'. They are in fact up to 30 per cent pure sugar – hardly an ideal way to start the day. Nutrification has even been extended to sugar itself. In countries from El Salvador to Zambia, sugar is fortified with vitamin A as a way to reduce child blindness and mortality. Meanwhile, in Australia, sugar with a low glycaemic index branded as LoGiCane™ has been devised to appeal to dieters.[42] Yet, in both these cases, the detrimental effects of the initial foods remain largely intact while more desirable changes to dietary patterns may be altogether discouraged.

The food policy scholar Gyorgy Scrinis sees this obsession with functional foods and those ingredients mentioned previously, such as TASTEVA®, as part of an ideology of 'nutritionism'.[43] This is based on a reductive understanding of nutrients which de-contextualizes them from the food, diets and eating practices in which they are embedded. More holistic and comprehensive changes are thus sacrificed as people undertake the unending task of changing what they ingest one nutrient at a time: this week more vitamin B, next week a little less fructose.

Something to this effect was borne out in the United States when sugar became a vilified ingredient in the 1990s, thanks to the predominance of the Atkins Diet. Food manufacturers thus switched to using more HFCS in their products instead, but then reversed back in the mid-2000s when 'low-carb' foods like yoghurts became the fashion and sugar was needed to bulk them out. Even as far back as 1913, the editorial of the *Journal of the American Medical Association* complained about such mixed messages on sugar published in the media: '[T]he hygienic preaching in the public columns is sometimes neither orthodox nor rational; and not infrequently it is tinged with the evident desire to produce a telling impression, which seems to be the fundamental aim of modern distributors of news and literature.'[44]

Returning to the role of the state, it should be noted that, while capitalist organizations are reluctant to accept generalized restrictions on commodified consumption, this does not mean that they are against regulation per se. Alongside the use of legal statutes to create barriers to entry, sugar producers the world around have also benefited from government mandates and other public policies that have built market demand for biofuel consumption.

In 2013, there were sixty-two mandates in place, many of which explicitly targeted sugar-beet and sugar-cane production by requiring fuel distributors to blend a certain amount of ethanol into their petrol supplies. Some of these mandates exist at the national level – the most important being the Brazilian requirement for a minimum 20 per cent ethanol content – and some at the sub-national level, such as those put in place by New South Wales and Maharashtra, both cane-growing regions.

Sugar producers, and in particular the milling companies, have been vocal proponents of this support. In the United Kingdom, representatives from British Sugar have stressed the need for biofuels to benefit from higher tax rebates so as to create 'a period of stability and clear direction for biofuels . . . [to] deliver the greenhouse gas emissions reduction goals agreed by the government'.[45] Contrast this with their approach towards higher taxes on sugar, for which the government also has consumption targets in the form of dietary guidelines: 'There is no conclusive evidence that a sugar tax would have the desired effect on consumer behaviour . . . We believe instead that the public would benefit from a better overall understanding of what constitutes a healthy, balanced diet by providing them with accurate information based on facts and science.'[46]

Such ideological inconsistency is to be expected. Businesses lobby on the basis of self-interest and will happily offer contradictory recommendations as long as they create a more conducive regulatory environment. But in terms of governing consumption in the interests of society, inconsistent policy is problematic. And there is plenty of inconsistency around. Notably, while government proposals to *reduce* sugar consumption have generated many media headlines, what has been less commented on is the fact that many states have continued to intervene in the sugar market in order to *widen* consumption.

These policies have included exemptions for sugar from value-added tax (in the United Kingdom), subsidized sales in public distribution systems (in India), and guaranteed state rations (in Cuba).[47] State-directed provisioning can even be found at the international level. In 2012, the UN World Food Programme spent US$17 million on sugar to disburse as emergency food aid in places including Syria and Djibouti. In each of these cases, sugar was given special treatment because it was considered an essential foodstuff that poor and endangered people should still be able to acquire. So with this example, we are taken back to the central political problem with which we started the chapter: on what basis should an individual's sugar consumption be the concern of others?

## Conclusion

The enduring commercial utility of sugar has been in dissolving barriers to accumulation. Whether it is by suspending shelf-life, modifying mealtimes or encouraging overeating, the properties of sucrose have been extremely useful in helping industrial food manufacturers to subvert the natural and cultural rules governing what can be eaten, when and in what quantities. Thus, it is not simply the profitability of sugared foods that accounts for the popularity of this ingredient but its ability to help manufacturers reshape society and continually *extend* the market in which their commodities can circulate. In this quest, their endeavours have been aided by political decisions to remove certain trade and investment restrictions, protect brands through intellectual property law and exclusive licensing agreements, treat issues of public health as private responsibilities and guarantee sugar's availability where necessary. In short, the pervasiveness of sugar has been purposely created.

The consequences of this mass sweetening have mapped onto various hierarchies of inequality. Understood in class terms, cheap sugar has increased labour exploitation by acting as a brake on wage inflation, lowering the costs of workers' subsistence calorific energy needs and providing a readily accepted alternative to more expensive and nutritious diets. The intersection of class and race has also made dependence on industrial foods a particular problem for minority groups. Acquiescence to this system has been secured through the advertising dreams sold by these products. These have given successive generations their reasons to put political faith in the consumer society as it represents, among other things, a liberating force from state socialism and a means of experiencing intimacy in an individualistic world. This consumerism has in turn depended on mobilizing the purchasing power of women as chief food providers, as well as enrolling children as autonomous market agents and encouraging them to spend money on sugary foods directly or make demands upon their carers (again, most likely women) to do so for them.

Finally, the health burden associated with the habitualization of sugar consumption has tended to fall on poorer communities, exacerbating existing racial and ethnic inequalities, and, in contributing to the production of disease, it has served as a mechanism of redistribution from taxpayers and health insurance policy holders to pharmaceutical companies and healthcare providers. In poorer countries of the world, where diabetes alone has doubled in the last thirty years, the internationalization of sweeter diets has been soured further by the uneven capacity to manage chronic disease and prevent early death. Looking forward, scrutiny of sugar as a drug food will surely only increase and, with it, scrutiny also on the political arrangements that have made it so pervasive within the global diet. The most important of these, as we shall see in the next chapter, relate to international trade.

CHAPTER THREE

# Terminal Trade Dependency

In 2011, the international trade in sugar was worth more than US$39 billion. This made sugar the fourth most valuable agricultural commodity traded in the world economy behind soybean, wheat and palm oil. It is perhaps no surprise that it is these commodities, along with corn, which underpin the general thrust towards greater consumption of meat, refined carbohydrates, vegetable oils and sweeteners. Economic interest in these ingredients has led distant lands to be re-inscribed in the world market as low-cost suppliers: masses of soybean are exported from Argentina, wheat from Kazakhstan, palm oil from Indonesia and sugar from Brazil. But, as we saw in the previous chapter, there have also been attempts to reorganize production and provide alternative sources of sweetener. Various ways of manufacturing these – and indeed animal feed, refined flour and vegetable oil – have been pursued so as to retain farm jobs and food production in the domestic economy. Different crop combinations thus serve up similar 'western' diets. Wheat, canola and sugar cane are predominant in Australia; wheat, rapeseed and sugar beet in the United Kingdom; and corn, soybean and both sugar crops in the United States.

Given these possibilities, this chapter looks at how the sugar trade is organized via state regulations, corporate relations and market routines. At the outset, it is important to note that, despite the multi-billion dollar *inter*national trade, most sugar is actually traded *intra*-nationally. According to 2011 FAO data, just 37 per cent of sugar was sold across national borders. Most sugar stayed within the country in which it was produced, typically because of the higher prices and lower transport costs available domestically. This indicates immediately the importance of government policy in shaping the markets within which the sugar commodity circulates.

For those producers that do export sugar – many of which are based in poor areas of the Global South – another important factor in price formation is whether the sugar is sold via the world market or trade agreements which give it preferential access to other domestic markets. For example, thanks to their preferential access to the EU and US markets respectively, in 2011 Mauritius earned US$865 per tonne of raw sugar exported, and Mexico US$795. By contrast, exporting largely to the world market, Guatemala earned just US$503 per tonne.[1] A final dimension of price formation relates to the type of sugar traded, refined sugar typically commanding a premium of around 10–20 per cent over raw sugar. So, in terms of trade, decisions have to be taken about how much to trade, with whom, at what price and in what type of sugar. In this respect, state elites managing the national economy have had to balance competing concerns, one of the most important being long-term reliance on others for either the *purchase* or *sale* of sugar. Whether such terminal trade dependency makes sense is one of the enduring political questions of the global sugar economy, a question we turn to now.

## Trade policy and the terms of competition

The importance of trade policy to the production of sugar is evident throughout its history. Perhaps most famous is the constellation of policies underpinning the colonial 'triangle trade' which saw manufactured goods like cloth and arms sold from Europe to Africa, slaves shipped from Africa to the Americas, and sugar and tobacco sent from the Americas back to Europe. This circulation of commodities across the Atlantic Ocean was mercantilist in orientation, and the terms of competition stacked in favour of those loyal to the crown.

Under the 1651 English Navigation Act, planters in the English colonies were compelled to ship their raw sugar to ports in England and to buy their slaves from English merchants, while subsequent legislation taxed foreign sugar imports at double the rate its own traders were charged. Following suit from the English, in 1664 the French government passed a similar tariff act to attract the sugar of the French Caribbean islands exclusively to French ports and exclude the entry of Dutch East Indies sugar. Anglo-centric and Franco-centric circuits were thus created alongside one another, and, despite their mercantilist orientation, tied together economic activities around the globe in such a way as to lay the foundation for a truly integrated capitalist world market to emerge.

The contemporary history of the international sugar trade has been marked by two attempts to do just that and transcend the legacies of mercantilism by liberalizing trade through multilateral negotiations. To a greater and lesser extent, both of these failed. The first concerned the period just after the Second World War, when the United States was leading the reconstruction of the capitalist world market by establishing international organizations to provide credit to war-torn allied economies. However, the organizations designed to oversee trade rules and prevent a return to the protectionist policies witnessed during the inter-war period failed to materialize. Plans for a 'World

Food Board' to stabilize agricultural prices and maintain emergency stocks and for an international trade organization that would link trade liberalization to full employment were both rejected by American politicians keen to defend the country's policy autonomy.

Despite their differences, both these proposals rested on the idea that trade should be managed through internationally negotiated state intervention. In other words, society could not rely on market mechanisms to prevent hunger and unemployment. What the United States eventually put in their place was the 1947 General Agreement on Tariffs and Trade (GATT), which was explicitly written to accommodate the import tariffs, export subsidies and protectionist 'trade remedies' of the American farm sector. In this way, the United States endorsed the principle of managed agricultural markets but roundly rejected its internationalist application.

The GATT was meant only as an ad hoc negotiation forum but eventually became the organization through which countries in the capitalist bloc would engage in reciprocal reductions of trade barriers throughout the Cold War. Yet, since it had excluded agriculture from its very inception, for the next four decades it did little to liberalize western farm policy. As far as sugar was concerned, the international trade would instead be governed by a series of exclusive hub and spoke arrangements offering, on the one hand, restricted market access to favoured countries, and, on the other, periodic international agreements to control prices for the rest. For free traders, as mentioned in this book's introduction, these arrangements both limited genuine competition and encouraged government intervention, preventing low-cost sugar producers from benefiting from export sales.

The second attempt to subject sugar to a more liberal

trade regime took place from the mid-1980s onwards with the formation of the World Trade Organization (WTO). This emerged out of the Uruguay Round of negotiations of the GATT and rested on a 'grand bargain' whereby developed countries would reduce tariffs on agriculture and labour-intensive manufactured goods like textiles and developing countries would liberalize access to services and strengthen their intellectual property and investment law. Given the historical resistance to liberalizing the international sugar trade – the unilateral free trade policy of Britain in the late nineteenth century aside – it is worth asking why sugar, along with other strongly protected products like rice and cotton, was included in international trade negotiations this time around.

One part of the answer is that many agricultural exporters such as Australia, Brazil, Canada, South Africa and Thailand had an offensive interest in liberalization and had come together as the Cairns Group to push for the inclusion of agriculture in the WTO. For agricultural importers, meanwhile, the costs of supporting domestic farm production were becoming politically untenable. In the European Community (EC), for example, expenditure on sugar had increased fivefold between 1980 and 1986.[2] Finally, and perhaps most importantly, state elites in the developed countries were unwilling to lose valuable export opportunities in sectors like pharmaceuticals and telecommunications for the sake of protecting sugar and other sensitive agricultural and manufacturing industries. For the grand bargain to go ahead, farmers would readily be sacrificed on the altar of free trade.

In the end, a deal was done. An Agreement on Agriculture, along with agreements on other sectors and a dispute settlement mechanism to solve any conflicts, came into force in 1995 with the establishment of the WTO. The main achievements of the Agreement on Agriculture as far as sugar was concerned were to reduce export subsidies (which the EC had been using excessively), establish a process for binding and reducing import tariffs, and create a minimum level of market access that all countries had to offer. However, the text also allowed significant wiggle room. It exempted counter-cyclical and income subsidies from cuts as long as they were decoupled from production. It also enabled tariffs to be bound at high and prohibitive levels, and allowed additional duties, known as safeguards, to be applied if and when imports of sugar and sugar-containing products fell below a certain price.

The effect of all this was to stall multilateral liberalization of the sugar trade by allowing various forms of protectionism to continue. In 1995, a World Bank study had put average bound tariffs for raw sugar in importing countries at 117 per cent, meaning it was made more than twice as expensive through taxation. It was anticipated that even by 2004, almost ten years after the establishment of the WTO, the figure would still be as high as 98 per cent.[3]

Yet the fact that the fabled 'level playing field' had not been brought into existence (if indeed it ever could be) does not mean that trade flows remained unchanged. The next section discusses two connected stories that have unfolded in the decades since the WTO was established – the rise of Brazil and the decline of the EU as respective export powers – and shows the different ways in which global capitalism has unfolded through the circulation of sugar.

*The rise and decline of sugar exporters*
In 1994, Brazil and the EU were both net exporters of sugar, selling over 3 million tonnes to the world market, placing them just behind Australia as the world's biggest

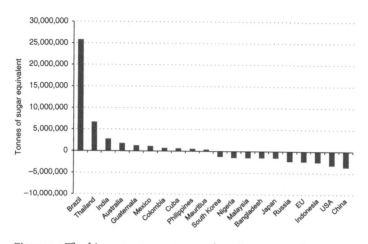

Figure 3.1 The biggest net exporters and net importers of sugar, 2011

*Note*: Positive values indicate net exports, negative values imports. Sugar equivalent includes raw and refined sugar but excludes ethanol.

*Source*: FAOSTAT.

sugar exporters. Over the next two decades, however, they would move in completely opposite directions. As detailed in Figure 3.1, Brazil increased its export levels significantly and now completely dominates the international market, exporting over 25 million tonnes in 2011. Meanwhile, the EU, partly from expanding to include new countries and partly due to trade-induced reforms, has so contracted its production of sugar that it became a net importer, buying 2.4 million tonnes from outside the bloc in 2011.

The export of Brazilian sugar has been spurred by increased consumption in countries including China, which bought more than US$1 billion worth of sugar in 2012–13, plus Egypt, Russia, Algeria, Bangladesh and Malaysia which imported over US$0.5 billion each – mainly raw sugar which was then refined domestically.[4] From the

Brazilian perspective, this has been an important source of effective demand for their sugar-cane industry, as have the extra 50 million people added to the country's own population since 1990 and their steadily rising life expectancy (or, put another way, ability to eat extra sugar).

In addition to these food markets, the demand for sugar-cane ethanol has also grown. While some of this has come from exports – Brazil sold more than US$1.5 billion worth to the United States in 2012–13, assisted by the removal of a tariff that had once protected American corn ethanol from imports – most has been sold domestically. It has gone into the tanks of the 'flex-fuel' cars that can run on pure ethanol and ethanol–petroleum blends and which now account for the majority of the country's vehicle fleet. Thus, the increase of sugar-cane production in Brazil was not driven by liberalization of heavily protected sugar markets in the EU, the United States and Japan, as envisaged at the outset of the WTO. Instead, it was the extra demand created by nutrition transition in rapidly industrializing countries and state-managed fuel substitution domestically which provided the markets necessary for expansion.

The flow of sugar and ethanol out of the Brazilian sugar-cane industry has been linked to a flood of capital into it. Increasing the capacity of sugar mills and bringing extra land under sugar-cane cultivation is an expensive business, costing hundreds of millions in US dollars. During the early 2000s, in the context of cheap global credit and high expectations, Brazilian mills loaded up on debt and began to make huge investments. Some opted to sell shares in their company, while others went in for mergers with foreign corporations. Some did both, such as the milling group Cosan which floated on the New York Stock Exchange in 2007 and then signed a joint venture agreement with Royal Dutch Shell in 2010 to form sugar-energy company Raízen, now the fifth-largest company by revenue in the whole of Brazil.

Such strategies led to a virtual takeover of the sector by foreign capital, as international agro-traders like Bunge and Louis Dreyfus and agro-processors like Tereos collectively acquired control over one-third of the country's milling capacity during the 2000s. During this period, many mills also borrowed heavily from either the state-owned Brazilian Development Bank or private commercial banks, both of which were encouraged to lend to the expanding sugar-cane sector by the Brazilian government. Marking a return to the 1970s, when the Brazilian state pumped huge amounts of money into the sugar-cane sector as part of its Proálcool biofuel programme to cut the oil import bill and bolster sugar prices, the anti-slavery group Repórter Brasil estimated that, between 2008 and 2010, the Brazilian Development Bank funded more than ninety sugar-ethanol projects with cheap credit to the tune of US$7.6 billion.

This was a boom time in sugar cane. Profits were running high and a mountain of equity and debt finance had been taken on to build future production capacity. However, after the boom there comes a bust and Brazil was no exception. As more and more sugar cane was harvested every season, downward pressure began to be put on sugar prices, squeezing the margins for producers. At the same time, the market for ethanol was dampened as the Brazilian government tried to protect Brazilian drivers (and voters!) from inflation by keeping the price of petrol down. Then, between 2011 and 2013, the amounts of sugar cane harvested actually fell, influenced by adverse weather conditions and an inability to replant cane fields because of tightening credit in the aftermath of the global financial crisis. The result was that the collective debt of Brazilian millers increased even further, reaching US$28 billion by

2014.[5] The trade association representing the country's biggest millers, UNICA, called this 'the greatest crisis in their history'.[6]

In this context, many mills were no longer able to roll over their debt by borrowing afresh and so were either mothballed or sold off. To make a comparison, at the peak of the sugar-cane boom in 2008, thirty new processing facilities were brought on stream; between 2011 and 2014, at least twelve every year were left to idle, creating ghost towns around the country as thousands of workers were laid off. Meanwhile, the concentration of ownership in the sugar-cane industry continued apace as the more solvent milling companies were able to buy up competitors on the cheap, many of which faced forcible sale under bankruptcy proceedings. Even new investors were not immune: Bunge put its loss-making sugar operations up for sale just a few years after acquiring them. Others decided that vertical integration offered greater safety as indicated by the joint venture between milling group Copersucar and trading firm Cargill, which together made them the world's biggest sugar-trading entity.

As well as redistributing wealth within the industry, this concentration also enabled tighter policy coordination and greater class consciousness on the part of milling capital. It is no coincidence that it was during this period of rapid expansion and contraction that UNICA began to exert greater influence. During the boom, they lobbied against ethanol tariffs in the EU and United States via offices in Brussels and Washington, DC and brought together industry elites with politicians and civil servants in Brasilia under the banner of the 'More Ethanol Movement'. During the bust, they successfully pushed the federal government to increase taxes on petrol to make ethanol more competitive in the domestic market *and* provide rebates on sugar and ethanol exports which effectively lowered their taxes by an estimated US$395 million per year.[7]

The emergence of Brazil as the world's major sugar exporter, then, cannot be understood as a straightforward story of a national industry steadily growing year on year. It has been indelibly marked by the see-saw motion of capitalism and the ways in which corporations have expanded within and beyond national borders, shaped, of course, by state regulations and interventions.

This approach is also useful for thinking about the swing in the EU's status from net sugar exporter to net sugar importer. In the EU, sugar had traditionally been regulated through a combination of guaranteed domestic prices, border tariffs and export subsidies. In 1975, an agreement had been made with former British colonies – including Mauritius, Fiji, Guyana, Jamaica and Swaziland – to import a fixed amount of sugar for Tate & Lyle's refineries that would also be sold at the higher domestic price. This locked the interests of the European sugar-beet producers and preferential African, Caribbean and Pacific (ACP) sugar-cane exporters together and their delicate balance persisted for decades, with the EU engaging in the rather bizarre business of both importing and exporting millions of tonnes of sugar each year. What finally ruptured this system was attributed to two trade reforms which meant that imports and exports, and thus domestic prices, could no longer be as carefully controlled.

The first of these reforms was the Everything But Arms agreement in 2001, in which the EU unilaterally offered duty-free and quota-free access to all exports (apart from weapons) from the Least Developed Countries – some of which had the potential to become much bigger sugar exporters. This created a first crack in the tariff wall protecting the EU sugar market. The second reform came out of a case brought by Australia, Brazil and Thailand to the WTO's Dispute Settlement Body. In this case the complainants argued that EU farmers and processors were able to export millions of tonnes of sugar to the world market only because they were cross-subsidizing from the high margins earned on their domestic sales. The WTO courts agreed that this was indeed a violation of the EU's commitment to limit subsidized exports to 1.3 million tonnes and thus the EU had to find another way to remove this surplus sugar from the market lest it drive down prices and put many producers out of business.

In the event, the EU did the job itself. In 2006, after much internal wrangling, the European Commission decided not to reduce the size of the production quotas that it allocated to individual countries but to lower the reference price by 36 per cent instead, making higher-cost production economically untenable. At the same time, the EU also renounced its agreement with the ACP exporters, much to their anger, and effectively made continued access to the EU sugar market at preferential rates (at least for those countries that did not qualify for the Everything But Arms agreement) conditional on signing more comprehensive free trade agreements.

Again, as with the decision to submit agriculture to the disciplines of the multilateral trading system, there were powerful interests within the EU in opening up the sugar trade. The EU Trade Commission was keen to strengthen its hand in WTO negotiations by showing that it had (ultimately) stuck to its Uruguay Round promises to limit export subsidies and had even made further concessions in agricultural market access. By helping to turn the EU's traditional preferential trade agreements with the ACP countries into reciprocal free trade agreements, meaning those where both sides agree to liberalize, sugar reform also meant that the EU no longer had to ask its fellow WTO members for an exemption. Non-reciprocal trade agreements ran counter to the rules they had collectively signed up to so, if it continued to give special treatment to some poor countries, the EU would have had to pay off others lest it find itself in the dock of the Dispute Settlement Body once again.[8] Finally, reform was good news for food manufacturers, who had for a long time lobbied for unfettered access to cheaper sugar. Indeed, the EU Trade Commission had been explicit in its strategy to shift the EU from an exporter of simple commodities like sugar to one of 'value-added' goods like processed food, which would be made easier if its manufacturers could access ingredients like sugar at lower prices.

The effects of this watershed reform were felt unevenly. More than 7 billion euros was made available as a kind of redundancy package to encourage *European* farmers and processors to exit the industry as quickly as possible, and thereby save political elites from the difficult task of enforcing compulsory closure. Between 2005 and 2012, the number of beet factories in the EU fell from 189 to 106, with those in Europe's periphery worst affected. And, as happened in Brazil, contraction led to concentration.

The EU's four big sugar-beet processors – Südzucker, Nordzucker, Tereos and British Sugar – have increased their share of EU production to around 60 per cent since reform. Partly this is down to the fact that production has been less affected in their 'home' countries of Germany, France and the United Kingdom than elsewhere, but it also reflects their expansion into other territories. For example, in 2014 the EU's biggest sugar-beet producer, the German-based Südzucker, had 29 factories in countries which included France, Belgium and Poland; the second biggest, Nordzucker, had ten in countries including Denmark,

Poland and Slovakia. Moreover, some had invested in those countries now eligible to export sugar back to the EU, effectively offshoring their production. The French company Tereos expanded into Mozambique, while the parent company of British Sugar, Associated British Foods, acquired a controlling stake in Africa's biggest sugar company Illovo.

Although such expansion is often justified on the basis that it leads to a more price-competitive industry, it is worth bearing in mind that EU sugar production does still benefit from a range of state subsidies. The most important of these is an income support paid directly to farmers. By way of example, in 2014 the UK government set this at £195 per hectare.[9] Based on an average beet holding of 30 hectares, this equated to £5,850 per British sugar farmer.[10] For those sugar farmers that remain in business, then, this income support has helped to offset the lower market price they now receive for their crop. Any increase in the competitiveness of the EU sugar processors that has resulted from reform must be seen within the context of an active farm-welfare policy.

Moreover, there is a considerable danger that the concentration of ownership that has resulted will allow these companies to collude and manipulate prices for their own pecuniary gain, thereby reducing the social benefits of having lower costs of production. In 2014, the German competition authorities fined Südzucker, Nordzucker and another German sugar processor 280 million euros for price fixing, while that same year a complaint was filed to the UK competition authorities by a distributor alleging that British Sugar was forcing it to pay over the odds for its sugar. This followed on from an exposé the previous year in which its parent company, Associated British Foods, was accused by the charity ActionAid of paying virtually no corporation tax in the poverty-stricken country of Zambia, saving its new acquisition Illovo millions of pounds. It did this through a combination of transfer pricing, investment-related tax breaks and legal challenges to the tax bracket assigned to it by the government. This should not be seen as a victimless exercise. George Sumatama, a head teacher in a government-funded school in the Zambian sugar-belt had this to say: 'Our school has no windows, doors or floors. Over a thousand children have to fit into just 12 classrooms, sitting in shifts and taught by 20 teachers. I think companies operating in Zambia should be paying more [tax] than they currently pay.'[11]

For those ACP sugar-cane exporters, meanwhile, a much smaller fund of 1.3 billion euros was made available by the EU. Unlike the assistance offered to European producers, this was not given directly to the companies affected but was managed by the EU as an 'Aid for Trade' package. Many of these countries were extremely dependent on sugar-cane exports. For some, like St Kitts and Nevis and Trinidad and Tobago in the Caribbean, the EU market was so important that reform sounded the death knell for the industry altogether, entire islands quitting cane after centuries of cultivation. Anticipating such upheaval when the price cuts were announced, the chief executive of the Caribbean Sugar Association, Ian McDonald, called them 'outrageous' and a betrayal of sugar farmers in the ACP. Once the cuts became a reality though, his attention – like that of other industry elites in the ACP – switched to getting as much of the aid as quickly as possible to cope with the changes.[12]

As Table 3.1 shows, of all those countries where sugar made up at least 10 per cent of their agricultural export profile in 2011, ten of these were integrated one way or another into the EU's system of preferential market access. In Swaziland, which received 134 million euros of the total

Table 3.1  Percentage share of sugar in total agricultural export earnings, 2011

| Country | Per cent | Country | Per cent |
|---|---|---|---|
| Swaziland* | 56 | Jamaica | 18* |
| Cuba | 52 | Mozambique | 18* |
| Guyana* | 41 | Guatemala | 14 |
| Fiji* | 26 | Dominican Republic | 13* |
| Belize* | 25 | El Salvador | 13 |
| Zambia* | 20 | Barbados | 12* |
| Brazil | 19 | Nicaragua | 10 |
| Malawi* | 19 | Thailand | 10 |

Note: * refers to those countries that have preferential access to the EU market. List does not include refining and re-export destinations.

Source: FAOSTAT.

Aid for Trade package, a decision was taken at the time of reform to try and make the industry more competitive so that it could offset the reduced price of sugar in the EU by exporting greater volumes. What this meant in practice was the loss or outsourcing of 4,400 mill jobs and retrenchment of healthcare and education services as the two milling companies 'rationalized' costs.

At the same time, though, 1,200 smallholder farmers funded by EU aid were enmeshed within the sugar-cane complex to provide extra cane for the mills to crush (unlike in Brazil, the mills in Swaziland could not buy up additional land themselves but had to bring it under cultivation via existing land-users). Much EU money also went to road-building projects in order to reduce transport costs to and from the mills, one of which, Ubombo, was now majority-owned by Associated British Foods, which in effect benefited twice over from EU assistance. The take-home point here is that the uneven effects of trade liberalization are felt within countries as well as between them, caused by the internationalization of ownership and the ways in which production is organized.

## Sugar highs and sugar lows

The last section showed the ways in which rising or falling prices, or even just expectations about them, could shape investment and trade dynamics, which then fed back into processes of price formation. This dialectical relationship that capitalists have to the market – responding to prices and in turn changing them again – is well known in the sugar industry. A glance at Figure 3.2 tells us why. The world market price has been notoriously volatile, encouraging export-led expansion during moments of soaring prices and undercutting it during periods of dwindling prices. The boom and bust experienced in Brazil since the mid-2000s has in fact been repeated around the world. As the sugar trader Czarnikow noted in 2013: 'The price of sugar remains below the total cost of production for most producers who supply the world market. The sale of sugar below operational cost of production, rising levels of debt and insolvency all highlight the damage that low prices have done.'[13]

This is one reason why headlines about high sugar prices must be taken with a pinch of salt: they often fail to remind us that prices go down as well as up (and quite often stay down). Another reason is that they do not report the *real* price of sugar, adjusted for inflation. In 2011, the nominal price of sugar peaked at US$0.60 per kg., one of the highest points it had ever reached. 'Sweet sugar hikes FAO food price index,' reported MercoPress at the time.[14] One might conclude that sugar prices were out of control and the era of cheap food well and truly at an end. However, long-term

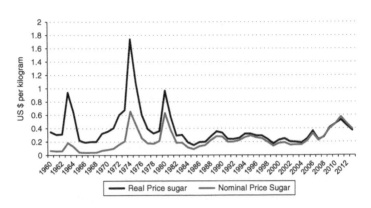

Figure 3.2 Annual price of sugar on the world market, 1960–2013
Source: World Bank Global Economic Monitor Commodities.

observers of the sugar market would rightly reply that this was the same price in real terms as in 1964. From the point of view of sugar exporters, this means that, unless the price of sugar runs well ahead of the rate of inflation, which is simultaneously pushing up their input costs, they are unlikely to see a major difference in gross margins. Contrary to what the nominal price suggests, business was far better in 1963 (with a real price of US$0.94 per kg.) than in 2013 (US$0.39 per kg.).

Although the meaning of price changes can be contested, their importance cannot. This goes for their effects on the food manufacturers and consumers who ultimately buy the sugar, as well as on the producers and traders that sell it. Indeed, after years of criticizing the low prices of sugar and other agricultural products for condemning farmers in poor countries to poverty, in the mid-2000s scholars of international development suddenly inverted their position and said that high prices were the problem. This was the argument that sudden price rises had caused a 'food crisis' by pushing up the price of imported crops and forcing millions of poor people to the threshold of starvation.

While most commentators tended to focus on the prices of staple commodities like corn and wheat, for consuming publics the price of 'luxury' commodities like sugar were also matters of grave importance. In Algeria, which was highly dependent on imports of sugar and vegetable oil, riots broke out across the country in 2011 over price increases for these commodities. In a bid to cling on to power, the Bouteflika government, already besieged by popular protest in the context of the Arab Spring, responded immediately by slashing import taxes and later provided consumer subsidies on these foods. Other protests over sugar prices that year – from Bolivia to Ethiopia – indicate the far-reaching effects of world market movements.

The reasons for the increase in commodity market prices, including sugar, have been hotly debated. Some focused on disruptions in supply caused by adverse weather and poor harvests. Lloyd's insurance group, for example, said rising sugar prices were influenced by projections of weaker monsoons in India and irregular rains in Brazil.

Others focused on demand-side explanations, namely the rapid growth of sugar consumption in Asia and Africa, and the surge in biofuel production, particularly from Brazilian sugar cane and American corn. A report for the UN Committee on World Food Security concluded that 'the introduction of a rigid biofuel demand does affect food commodity prices' because government targets keep demand for agricultural crops ahead of available supply and any increase in the oil price means that producers move even more of their crops into the fuel market. Providing econometric evidence to this effect, a model developed by the OECD-FAO found that if global ethanol demand increased by 11 per cent, the world sugar price would increase by

4 per cent, essentially because Brazilian producers would divert sugar cane from the international sugar market and into the domestic biofuel market.[15]

Finally, some explanations drew attention to dysfunctions in commodity markets themselves. A report from UNCTAD, for example, argued that financial investors were 'pumping and dumping' assets for speculative purposes, moving short-term commodity prices away from what the supply and demand fundamentals of the 'physical trade' warranted.

There is a grain of truth in all these accounts. The world market price for sugar, like many market phenomena, is over-determined, meaning that it can be explained by more than one factor. In this sense, identifying precisely what caused the 2006–2011 price spikes is something of a fool's errand. The same was true in the 1970s and 1980s. The peaks were attributed variously to adverse weather, OPEC-induced rises in the oil price, panic buying and structural factors such as the residual nature of the world market.[16] The subsequent troughs were then attributed to appreciation of the dollar, substitution of sugar with HFCS, regulatory changes which encouraged sugar surpluses such as the EC reforms in the mid-1970s, and structural factors like the large sunk costs of sugar production.[17]

Arguably, then, what is more important than what caused certain price movements is what people *believe* caused them and the political decisions taken on this basis. In this next section, we examine some of the responses of state elites to fluctuating world market prices over the period 2005–2015, the first of which concerns the security of supply.

*State management*
Historically, when trade flows have been threatened, states have promoted domestic production and/or mercantile

trade arrangements to guarantee supply. As mentioned in the book's introduction, the sugar-beet industry in Europe in fact owes its very existence to the process of state-led import substitution. Nowadays, China is where some of the most important decisions on trade policy are being taken. China's rapid integration into the global capitalist system has seriously challenged the Chinese Communist Party's long-held policy of self-sufficiency in food, not least because of the country's unprecedented urbanization and nutritional transition. Imports of animal feed in the form of soybean have increased most markedly and in recent years even staple grains like rice and wheat have had to be imported to keep pace with demand. Consequently, concern about resource insecurity is palpable among China's leaders. That said, political scientist Shaun Breslin notes that, just because an overarching goal exists, it does not follow that the Chinese government has a unitary means of achieving it, nor that it is in complete control of the process. According to Breslin, even large state-owned enterprises tasked with buying farmland, food companies and agricultural commodities abroad in fact operate with considerable autonomy from the Chinese government.[18]

In its official policy, the Chinese government has sought to increase sugar supply from both national and international sources. In 2013–14, supply was split between sugar-cane producers, based mainly in the southern provinces of Guangxi and Yunnan (85 per cent), sugar-beet producers based mainly in the north (5 per cent) and raw-sugar imports from Brazil, Thailand and Cuba processed at its domestic refineries (10 per cent). To support domestic production, prices have been inflated through regular stockpiling by the national government and tariff and licensing controls placed on imports over the minimum amount that the country agreed to accept as a condition of joining the WTO in 2001. Opportunities to open the import market further – in the 2014 bilateral free trade agreement with Australia, for example – have also been refused. Given the limited availability of arable land in China, the government has also sought to increase production through intensive, rather than extensive, means. Foreign investment from Associated British Foods and the Thai company Mitr Phol have been permitted, designed to improve crop yield and processing efficiency in existing farms and factories.

In terms of the sugar it does import, the strategy has been to encourage direct ownership of foreign producers, rather than locking them into preferential trade agreements. In 2011, the China National Cereals, Oils and Foodstuffs Import and Export Company (COFCO), which has almost exclusive control over sugar imports into the country, bought the Australian producer Tully Sugar. In 2014, it followed this up by acquiring the agricultural trading division of Noble which owns sugar mills in Brazil. This gave COFCO the power to dictate whom these companies sell their sugar to, although, as noted above, the extent to which this really means control by the Chinese state is unclear. Although the majority of COFCO's shares are held by the state and the company clearly benefits from the country's trade policy, at the same time it is also a profit-making organization and readily works with private equity firms and other powerful shareholders in managing its portfolio of multinational corporations.

The stated intention of the Chinese Ministry of Commerce has thus been to 'guide companies to contribute to a more reasonable sugar-importing order for the sake of the long-term development and overall interest of the industry'.[19] However, this is easier said than done, given that too many imports quickly destabilize domestic price management. The Chinese government cannot have its cake and eat it.

As noted before, China has to import a minimum amount under WTO rules so, in terms of trade, it can only restrict levels beyond this amount. To protect domestic producers in times of difficulty, then, attention has turned instead to criminalizing petty traders for engaging in smuggling, a practice which is rife whenever sugar outside the country suddenly becomes much cheaper. Moreover, domestic supply management strategies such as stockpiling can only really defend prices in the short term since sooner or later the stocks will be released. This has encouraged state officials to squeeze down saccharin production so as to create extra demand for sugar from food manufacturers. Finally, while provincial officials in Guangxi and Yunnan have pushed for measures to support prices, national officials are also under pressure from officials in other (urbanized) quarters to make sure it does not become expensive, inflating food prices and leading factory workers to agitate for higher wages. All of this shows there is no prima facie 'national interest' when it comes to trade policy and that the politics of sugar are marked by divisions *within* nation-states as well as between them.

The second political question is directed more towards exporters of sugar, and asks how state elites should manage their relationship to the world market in the interests of national economic development. There is a rich body of theoretical work on this issue, among the most notable contributions coming from the Argentinian economist Raúl Prebisch. In the 1950s, he argued that, far from acting as an engine of development, exports of primary commodities like sugar had actually hindered poorer countries.[20] The reason was that these commodities suffered from declining terms of trade: over time, more and more had to be exported in order to pay for the same amount of manufactured goods imported from richer industrialized economies in the West. Because of this, Prebisch advised state elites to adopt programmes of import-substitution industrialization, directing attention away from the export of primary products and instead towards the building of domestic manufacturing capacity in industries like chemicals, machinery and motor vehicles.

However, Prebisch soon became disillusioned at the failure of countries that embraced this programme to stimulate high levels of autonomous growth. So he began to question not what was traded per se but the regulatory structure surrounding trade which contributed to the relative price decline of primary commodities. Among the reforms he proposed were regional trade agreements among poor countries, non-reciprocal tariff cuts by richer countries, and measures to ensure equitable and stable commodity prices. Other Third World radicals went even further, demanding the nationalization of property and creation of aggressive natural resource cartels modelled on OPEC. While aspects of this thinking can be discerned today – some in Brazil have voiced concern about the growing dependence on low-value agro-exports and 're-primarization' of the economy – the prevailing attitude within development policy circles has been to return to the principle of comparative advantage and accept one's 'natural' place in the international economy.

These different approaches can be seen in Cuba's economic history. As noted in the book's introduction, the sugar trade was influential at the very birth of its modern history. In 1955, a quarter of a million sugar workers had come out on strike after their wages had been slashed following a reduction in Cuba's international sugar quota and the decision by the United States to increase its own production. Foreshadowing later events, the strike had taken on insurrectionary proportions in some places as workers had seized town halls and clashed with the army. In fact, as Fidel Castro's guerrilla campaign gained momentum, even Castro reached out to the country's sugar mill owners and farmers for financial and political support, responding to their desire for better trade opportunities.[21]

Upon taking power in 1959, the revolutionary Cuban government at first moved cautiously, initially pledging to leave the sugar plantations in the hands of their current owners. But tensions with the United States soon grew, encouraged by the American decision in 1960 to further reduce Cuba's sugar import quota. Coupled with its belief that the country was too dependent on sugar, the Castro government suddenly launched a sweeping programme of nationalization, taking ownership of sugar mills, land and infrastructure and channelling the surplus into industrialization programmes.

Unfortunately for Castro, since sugar had been the country's main foreign exchange earner, this strategy created an acute balance of payments problem that crippled the economy. It was in this context that the Cuban leadership renewed its emphasis on sugar exports, but with a greater determination to tackle what Ernesto 'Che' Guevara, then Cuba's minister of industry, called 'the unequal balance of trade'.[22] Following Prebisch's intellectual evolution, Guevara argued that it was not dependence on sugar that was the problem, but the fact that time spent producing this commodity was valued less than time spent producing industrial commodities.

Since the United States had put an embargo on *all* trade with the island in 1961 and International Sugar Agreements were proving less than effective in managing prices, to reform the regulatory structure surrounding the sugar trade Cuba had little option but to turn to the USSR. Under a Communist trade pact, dubbed a 'socialist division of labour', Cuban sugar was traded for Soviet oil and industrial goods. Based on the prices these products were fetching in the open market, the historian Jorge Pérez-López estimated that this deal transferred a massive surplus to Cuba, somewhere in the region of US$18 billion between 1973 and 1984.[23] This gave Moscow significant political leverage over Havana although, by the same token, the arrangement also went some way towards funding the Cuban government's extensive provision of subsidized health care and education during this period.

When the Soviet Union imploded in the late 1980s, the Cuban sugar trade went with it. Imports of oil, fertilizers, pesticides and tractors suddenly dried up, leading to a drop not only in sugar production but in food production also. Export earnings fell precipitously and in 2002 the government had little choice but to decommission almost half the country's 156 sugar mills, allocate degraded former plantation land to other uses and try to find jobs for more than 200,000 newly redundant workers.

Rising world prices since the mid-2000s and softening attitudes towards foreign investment by Raul Castro, Fidel's successor, have hinted at a partial recovery for the industry (in 2012 the Brazilian construction firm Odebrecht became its first overseas investor since the revolution). Yet sugar has long since been replaced by remittances and tourism as the country's main source of foreign exchange. And to the extent it will contribute to the country's growth in the future, it is as likely to be in the form of heritage tourism – selling holidaymakers and the Cuban diaspora the culture of rum drinking and the history of plantation life – as in the form of raw sugar exports.

The third political question is one for both exporting

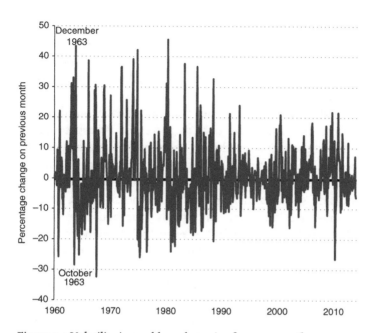

Figure 3.3 Volatility in world market price for sugar, 1960–2013

*Source*: World Bank Global Economic Monitor Commodities. Prices are in nominal cents.

and importing countries and concerns the control of price fluctuation. Figure 3.3 details the percentage change on last month's world market sugar price and shows that volatility has long been a problem. For instance, in October 1963 the price fell by 28 per cent; two months later, in December, it was up 43 per cent. For sugar producers dependent on export sales, this has created tremendous uncertainty. Along with the tendency for the world market price to reach levels below the cost of production, it explains why many sugar-exporting countries *want* to be locked into preferential trade agreements. This can be seen today in the support given by the Dominican Republic and the Philippines for continuation of the United States' preferential trade arrangements, in which, not coincidentally, they have two of the biggest quota allocations (the logic of shipping raw sugar 7,000 miles from Manila to California is otherwise hard to fathom).[24]

State elites have at times tried to manage world market prices directly. As far back as 1902, the British sought to protect their cane-producing colonies from subsidized beet sugar by bringing together major producers in Europe and making a collective agreement to apply import taxes on any subsidized sugar exports. The so-called Brussels Convention on sugar was hugely ambitious; anticipating the creation of the WTO, it even had its own Permanent Commission to monitor the use of government subsidies and resolve any trade disputes. In fact, the legal scholar Michael Fakhri regards it as the first truly multilateral trade institution.[25]

Later efforts to support the international sugar price were less intrusive of domestic politics but were no less determined to manage the market. Between 1931 and 1984, a series of international commodity agreements were negotiated that committed signatories to import/export specific quantities of sugar that would help keep prices within an agreed range. Indeed, one of them, the 1968 International Sugar Agreement, would be negotiated under the auspices of that committed trade interventionist Raúl Prebisch, then secretary-general of the United Nations Conference on Trade and Development.

As suggested in Figures 3.2 and 3.3, the International Sugar Agreements were hardly an unqualified success. Undermined by 'free rider' countries that stayed out of the agreements and continued to export as much and import as little as they liked, the very idea of international supply management soon lost credibility. Not only did this form of state regulation have its practical problems, it also jarred with the increasingly influential ideology of neo-liberalism, which sought to advance a more market-based and de-politicized form of capitalism.

Proponents of this, like the economists Donald Larson and Brent Borrell writing for the World Bank, argued that instead of relying on agreements negotiated by states to *remove* price uncertainty, sugar producers and food manufacturers would be better off accepting market fluctuations and using private risk management instruments to *offset* any untoward changes.[26]

Data from one of the major commodity exchanges, the Intercontinental Exchange in the United States, suggests their advice was followed.[27] In 1994, it oversaw the exchange of 5 million Sugar No. 11 contracts. This is an industry-standard contract for 50 long tonnes of raw sugar, which allows buyers or sellers to fix a future price for sugar in US dollars up to two years in advance. By 2011, this figure had jumped fivefold to 25 million. That same year, another popular contract for sugar, the White Sugar Futures contract for 10 tonnes, which is priced in Chinese yuan and sold on the Zhengzhou Commodity Exchange, was traded 128 million times.[28]

Along with contracts for corn and soy, sugar futures are among the most popular agro-financial assets. They are also, one would assume, among the most profitable. The paper value of all the No. 11 contracts traded in 2011, for example, was somewhere in the region of US$746 *billion*. It is referred to as paper value because most traders do not wish to buy or sell the physical commodity but simply make a small margin on the exchange of the paper contract. These traders are called speculators and they participate in the futures market alongside physical traders, known as hedgers. So the paper value of futures is a bit misleading in the sense that the full price of the contract is not paid, only the difference caused by movements in price in the meantime. Nevertheless, these can still add up to significant amounts, as legendary commodities investor Jim Rogers (net worth US$300 million) intimated in a 2013 interview: 'If you go to a restaurant tonight and there's sugar on the table, put it in your pocket. 'Cos it's free, and it's gonna go high!'[29]

But this has brought problems of its own, as we noted earlier. The expansion of sales in futures and other risk-management instruments like options (which allow parties to get out of their futures contract early if prices move in a favourable direction), as well as the invention of completely new products such as commodity index funds, have 'financialized' food. This means that sugar and other agricultural producers have become both more dependent on the services of financial intermediaries and more exposed to the effects of speculation.

Even some speculators have found this situation problematic. In 2010, a group representing sugar traders complained to the Intercontinental Exchange that prices were moving 10–20 per cent not just month to month but suddenly minute to minute. They claimed this was because of a new group of 'parasitic' high-frequency traders using senseless algorithms to execute decisions which had de-linked the exchange from reality at the expense of traditional market users like themselves.[30] In other words, rather than acting as a mechanism for discovering the 'proper' market price of sugar and allowing buyers and sellers to hedge against price fluctuations, the commodity exchange was becoming stuck in vicious feedback loops based on automated trading.

In terms of the wider political significance of this kind of contestation, we can conclude that, while direct regulation of the world sugar price itself remains unthinkable, intervention in the markets through which this price is formed seems increasingly permissible. Three years after the complaint to the Intercontinental Exchange, for example, its chief executive officer Jeffrey Sprecher was passing on the same advice, telling US senators that the rules that enabled high-speed trading needed to be overhauled. 'The markets are too complex,' admitted Sprecher.[31]

## Governing international trade

The argument made so far is that, whereas the international sugar trade used to be governed via commodity-specific and interventionist regulation, now it is dealt with under broader and more liberal arrangements designed to let goods and capital flow freely. However, the enduring problems facing buyers and sellers of sugar have not abated, meaning that demands for various forms of state protection and assistance have persisted also. This has shaped ongoing negotiations in the WTO where, despite the difficulties of agreeing and implementing agricultural reforms in the 1986–1994 Uruguay Round, members launched another negotiation round in 2001.

Struggling with the weight of its ambitious agenda to liberalize even more areas of the world economy, the Doha Round dragged on for more than a decade, although certain commitments were agreed upon along the way.

At the sixth ministerial meeting in 2005, and reflecting the approach the EU was taking in its domestic sugar reform, members agreed to eliminate export subsidies across the board, increase market access for Least Developed Countries, and provide 'Aid for Trade' funding. Work continued behind the scenes on the more difficult decisions of how to cut agricultural tariffs and subsidies, and, in 2008, a draft text was released which tried to provide some common ground. Essentially, this replicated the approach taken during the Uruguay Round: there were proposed cuts to tariffs with exemptions for 'sensitive products' and proposed cuts to subsidies with exemptions for income payments decoupled from production.

Biofuels were also the subject of a difference of opinion, although they were treated more decisively than other agricultural commodities when the EU and the United States immediately excluded them from the list of environmental goods scheduled for faster liberalization.[32] Environmental goods are those which in some way help to protect or restore ecological systems, a vague definition which leaves plenty of room to include some products and exclude others. As it was, ethanol would be treated within the WTO as an agricultural good and biodiesel as an industrial good, allowing states to place high tariffs on imports – especially for sugar-based ethanol.

Finally, at the ninth ministerial meeting in 2013, an agreement was made to increase trade by cutting 'red tape' at customs ports and to shield agricultural stockholding programmes in developing countries from WTO legal action. When and what decisions would be made around tariffs and subsidies was again left for another day.

Although it has been difficult for member states to use the WTO to push trade liberalization forward, they have been much more effective in preventing it from falling back. With respect to sugar, this can be seen in the use of the dispute settlement mechanism to challenge protectionist policy. This has not only been invoked by Australia, Brazil and Thailand in their case against the EU, but also by Colombia against Chile and, before they became members of the European Union, by Poland against Slovakia.

The intensified surveillance of trade policy enabled by

the WTO has also meant that many illegal subsidies are stopped before they take full effect. For example, in 2011 as sugar producers in the EU grew tempted by the favourable world market price, the Global Sugar Alliance, an ad hoc coalition of sugar exporters, warned the bloc not to renege on its previous commitments to limit export subsidies. Then again, in 2014, WTO members put pressure on India to remove its export subsidy, which had been put in place as an emergency measure to help sugar mills increase production and finally pay their rancorous cane farmers. In sum, as far as sugar and biofuels are concerned, the WTO has been much more successful in *re*-regulating production, by permitting only certain kinds of domestic farm support to be put in place, than in its supposed real mission to *de*-regulate trade by reducing tariffs and other barriers.

As noted before, though, multilateral liberalization at the WTO is not the only way in which trade policy can be reformed. Indeed, during the period in which the Doha Round has stalled, almost two hundred bilateral trade deals have been concluded. For the US government, the turn towards bilateralism can be seen as a reaction to the failure to conclude the WTO Doha Round and the Free Trade Area of the Americas, a regional trade agreement which was aborted in the mid-2000s. For US sugar producers, though, the turn towards bilateralism has meant more negotiations potentially undermining their system of domestic supply management.

In most cases, they have been successful in limiting the damage. In the free trade agreements with the Dominican Republic and Central American countries (ratified 2005), with Peru (2007), Colombia (2011) and Panama (2012), only small additional import allowances were granted. In the free trade agreement with Australia (2004), sugar was excluded from the deal altogether. However, in many respects the damage had already been done by the North American Free Trade Agreement (NAFTA) between the United States, Canada and Mexico, ratified in 1993.

Unable to keep sugar out of the agreement, in part because the powerful corn lobby was pushing for agricultural liberalization too, American producers could only manage to phase in the implementation of sugar reform slowly over fifteen years and, once that period was up, sponsor another piece of legislation which required surplus sugar to be turned into ethanol. For their part, Mexican sugar producers, squeezed in their domestic market by American exports of HFCS (which have grown *twenty-five* times over since NAFTA came into effect), now have unlimited access to the US sugar market.[33]

The upshot is that the system supporting sugar prices in the United States has become increasingly dependent on the goodwill of taxpayer-funded ethanol blending, the marketing decisions of Mexican sugar producers and the ability of the American sugar industry to elude one trade agreement after another. The latest cloud on the horizon in this respect is the Trans-Pacific Partnership, a trade and investment treaty mooted between fourteen countries in the Asia-Pacific region and which the American Sugar Alliance has typically opposed. They testified to the US International Trade Commission that any additional market access commitments for sugar in the agreement would 'severely damage the US [sugar] industry, generate large government expenditures, and make the US domestic sugar program unworkable' – almost exactly the same language it used in its testimony on the free trade agreement with Australia back in 2003.[34]

For individual capitals in the American sugar industry, one other option has been to position themselves to benefit from free trade if and when it comes about. To this end, it is notable that Florida Crystals Corporation, the sugar division of the conglomerate owned by billionaire Cuban exiles Alfonso and Jose Fanjul, has recently become the largest sugar refiner in the world. Since 2007, it has bought the Redpath Sugar refinery in Canada and the San Nicolas mill and refinery in Mexico (both NAFTA members) as well as Tate & Lyle's refineries in London and Portugal, and one of their major suppliers, Belize Sugar Industries.

This strategy of vertical integration has the advantage of providing both political influence in different states and economic protection from the vagaries of the world market. It is likely to be informed, too, by the recent experience of the Fanjuls in the Dominican Republic, who also own the country's biggest sugar exporter, Central Romana Corporation. Wikileaks cables revealed that in the run-up to the United States' free trade agreement with the Dominican Republic, American officials feared that a 'small, powerful coterie of infuriated sugar barons' would derail the deal because it would weaken their hold over trade between the two countries, especially in sweeteners. The cables report that the sugar barons were 'motivated and wealthy enough to purchase congressional votes wholesale' but, under pressure from free trade interests in the country (and the US government and the IMF, too), they finally acquiesced to the deal – though only after securing some additional tax concessions from the Dominican government in the process.[35] What this episode shows is the degree to which distinct policy arenas can be captured by the narrow interests of a particular fraction of capital. Notwithstanding the push back against the 'sugar barons', when it comes to trade policy, it would seem that state autonomy in the Dominican Republic is much more restricted than somewhere like China, where the government has considerably more leeway.

Vertical integration has been pursued by other sugar producers, too. In 2010, Wilmar International, the agricultural trading giant based in Singapore, bought the Australian company Sucrogen for US$1.5 billion and with it control of over half of Australia's raw sugar output. It later added more refining capacity in Australia and Indonesia as well as milling capacity in India and Myanmar. The two major shareholders in Wilmar are the agro-trader Archer Daniels Midland and the Kuok Group, the latter being the family business of the so-called 'sugar king' Robert Kuok, the second-richest man in South-East Asia.[36] Notably, just a year before Wilmar made its move, Robert Kuok had sold his Malaysian refineries to the country's government, unable to make as much profit given the rising price of raw sugar on the world market and the strict consumer price controls insisted upon by the state – illustrating again the close relationship between trade dynamics and investment decisions.

The effects of this restructuring have been twofold. First, it has tied together different production sites into a regional sugar-cane complex. As well as linking sugar mills and refineries around South-East Asia, Wilmar also announced plans to use the expertise it has now acquired in sugar-cane agriculture to develop new plantations back in Indonesia, where it is already a dominant force in palm oil production. In 2011, the Indonesian Refined Sugar Association, headed by a representative from Wilmar, said that the land would come from the area set aside by the government for conversion to agriculture. Conveniently, sugar cane was exempted from a recent moratorium on the conversion of forest and peat land to plantation monoculture.[37]

Second, restructing has further eroded the role of domestic institutions in managing the export trade. As recently as 1990, George C. Abbott could write that 'state agencies enjoy a virtual monopoly in the export trade. There are, in fact, very few private firms engaged in the sugar export business'.[38] This is no longer the case. Much to the anger of Australian cane farmers, the new foreign owners of the country's milling industry – Wilmar, COFCO and Mitr Phol, which took over MSF Sugar in 2012 – all decided to market their exports themselves and split from the Queensland Sugar Corporation. Up until 2006, this was a state-backed marketing board, meaning that it decided where all sugar exports from Queensland would be sold and at what price, a collective strength which benefited the industry as a whole. What the farmers feared was that export prices would be driven down as different producers were put in competition with each other and, specifically for those growing for Wilmar and COFCO, that there would be no transparency over how this price was set because these companies are essentially trading with themselves.

All in all, what we have witnessed in the two decades since the WTO came into existence and inaugurated a new era of global trade politics has been a decisive shift to new forms of state intervention, specifically, the provision of capital to favoured firms and the extension of market discipline to other countries. Interventions to delimit or re-purpose competition to support something other than lower consumer prices are, by contrast, harder to justify, both domestically and internationally.

For free traders, this is a positive development, albeit one that has yet to be fully realized as the legacies of post-war protectionism prove difficult to shake off. For state elites and sugar producers, the neo-liberal policy turn has been equivocal. It has enabled some businesses to expand, such as the export-led millers in São Paulo, and destroyed others by removing the barriers and supports which insulated them from low and uncertain prices. But even for those producers that have rallied behind free trade, as we saw with overproduction in Brazil and the takeovers in Australia, there have come times when they too have sought refuge in state interventionism. Moreover, producers in the EU and the United States have argued that low-cost exporters in developing countries unfairly benefit from lax regulation which provides them with cheaper labour and fewer environmental obligations. In other words, they have argued against liberalization on the basis that their would-be competitors' costs of production are under-priced. Putting the vested interests of the European and American producers aside, their underlying argument carries much force. For if we accept that *all* prices are political, then it becomes impossible in any objective sense to distinguish those government policies that 'distort' international trade from those policies that do not. This fractures the very foundation on which free trade advocates stand: the belief that trade-distorting policies can be singled out, and that once they are exorcised from the economy, comparative advantage alone will determine where production takes place.

There is also a moral reason to question the logic of liberalization and it resides in the fate of the hundreds of millions of people in the Global South in some way dependent on peasant agriculture, livestock herding, artisanal fishing and forest gathering. Mass-market sugar production, however it is organized ideologically, tends to be inimical to these traditional and often invisible economic activities as it takes away the natural resources necessary for their survival. Moreover, it is especially biased against women and ethnic and racial minorities, who are typically incorporated into sugar production and other highly capitalized industries on an adverse basis. Thus the dislocation and uneven development associated with the liberalization of the sugar trade cannot be understood solely with reference to changing fortunes in the sugar industry. It must also be seen in the context of what rural sociologist Philip McMichael calls a 'relentless assault on small farming' by expanding circuits of capital embodied in commodified farm inputs, footloose agrarian finance and surplus food dumping.[39] We return to these themes in the next two chapters.

## Conclusion

Historically, there have been key import and export poles around which the trade of sugar has flowed. The Atlantic triangle trade between Britain and its Caribbean colonies was one such circuit; the Cold War circuits around the United States and the USSR and their respective dependencies were others. In the contemporary period, and reflecting the shift in capitalist economic growth towards the Global South more generally, the sugar trade has become increasingly polarized by China and Brazil. In contrast to their predecessors, this circuit has been less exclusive and less shaped by the forces of imperialism and ideological struggle. However, this is not to say that the more pragmatic economic concerns that have animated the international sugar trade have been apolitical. The timeless tensions over how to manage security of supply, how to manage the economic surplus from sugar production and how to manage international price volatility are all still evident today – although they have been resolved in different ways.

One reason for this is because the way in which states are legally able and politically willing to support sugar production has changed. Intervention through trade measures has been made more difficult by rules constitutionalized in the WTO and in free trade agreements, leaving domestic policies like ad hoc loans and direct income payments as the most popular options to assist farmers, not least because states have been reluctant to interfere with the price nego-tiations between farmers and processors/millers directly.

There have also been developments in ownership that have an important bearing on who profits from trade. The fact that Europe-based capital has been invested in seven of the world's top ten sugar-producing companies reinforces the point made in the introduction that economic prosper-ity cannot be thought about in terms of discrete national industries. For instance, although most of the world's sugar is exported from Brazil, it is arguable that the benefits of this have not accrued primarily to the Brazilian population, or even its sugar-cane workforce, but to the shareholders, managers and salaried employees of its big corporations. For more detail on why this is the case, we need to know more about the way in which sugar is made – its mode of production – and how this has privileged some people over others.

# CHAPTER FOUR

# Exploiting and Expelling Labour

The chapter on trade argued that the forces of international competition are growing stronger and are shaping where in the world sugar is produced. But it left off by noting that if we want to understand who this actually benefits, we need to know more about *how* that sugar is produced. In terms of its effects on poverty reduction, sugar-cane production is of particular importance. As shown in Figure 4.1, this is grown in the tropics, an area either side of the equator which encompasses those countries that used to be collectively known as the Third World. Data from the International Fund for Agricultural Development shows that rural poverty is still widespread in many of these countries: 1,325 million people live on less than US$2 per day in the rural areas of Asia and the Pacific, 433 million in the rural areas of sub-Saharan Africa, and 24 million in the rural areas of Latin America and the Caribbean.[1]

For the millions of farmers and workers who labour in sugar-cane production, then, the crop provides a vital source of income. However, given the system of global capitalism within which sugar-cane production exists, there are pressures on individual producers to reduce costs and raise profits, even with a degree of government protection in place. This being so, even the most socially responsible companies are unlikely to pay their suppliers and employees much more than they have to. Nor are these pressures confined to sugar cane, the sugar crop most readily associated with

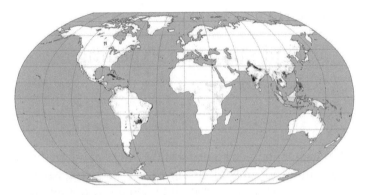

Figure 4.1 Global sugar-cane production, 2000

*Source*: University of Minnesota Institute on the Environment 2010 (Creative Commons).

media exposés about human rights abuses. As I soon show, the exploitation and expulsion of labour can be found in the sugar-beet industry, too. In short, capitalist social relations fundamentally condition (though do not determine) the kind of livelihoods that rural labourers get dealt, and it is with these relations that we must start our analysis.

## Factories in the field

In thinking about how capitalism conditions work-life, it is useful to imagine the sugar industry as factories in the field. In one sense, of course, this can be taken literally. Visit a sugar-cane mill or sugar-beet processor and you will have to drive past field after field of tall swaying grass or arable farmland before arriving at a large industrial unit, churning out smoke and surrounded by trucks delivering crops. Inside, it conforms to the stereotypical characteristics of factory production, complete with noisy conditions and often incredibly hot temperatures. The crops move along a production line chopped, crushed, boiled, spun and crystallized by various machines and are overseen by workers organized according to a strict division of labour.

But the idea of the factory system can also be taken out into the field itself. In order to keep transport costs down and prevent crops from drying out and losing sucrose content after they have been harvested, mills and processors are based in close proximity to the areas where the crop is grown. They also have to coordinate the cane and beet deliveries to make sure they receive a steady rate of raw material (too much and it begins to pile up at the factory gate; too little and the expensive fixed capital is under-utilized). This results in a centrally organized system of harvest and transportation, 'planned like a military operation' as the anthropologist D. W. Attwood put it.[2] Moreover, to assure supply and generate profits for their owners, farms themselves may even take on characteristics of the factory, the classic example being the plantation system of hired hands labouring under the watchful eye of an overseer. The historical rise of the sugar factory – harnessing steam power, operating 24 hours a day, constantly increasing capacity – has gone hand in hand with the extension of industrial discipline over agriculture itself.

In the Marxist tradition, capitalism is understood as the appropriation of 'surplus value' or unpaid labour from the workforce. How has this been increased through the factory farm? One strategy has been to make people work more. This can involve longer days, shorter breaks, the adoption of round-the-clock shift work and the intensification of work. The case of manual cane harvesters in Brazil shows how these techniques intertwine and the severe toll that they take. Firstly, rather than being paid a day-rate or salary, workers are paid a piece-rate according to how much cane they cut. Alongside this economic inducement, cultural norms are deployed that associate large harvests with masculine notions of strength and fortitude. These incentives to (over)work are supported by techniques to prevent under-work. The initial hiring process involves a long trial period in which those who cut less cane are not retained; for those who are kept on, transport to and from the fields at set times and the threat of unpaid suspension or not being rehired next season keeps workers from easing off.

Consequently, despite little change in the nature of the work – cane cutters still rely on swinging a machete to get the job done – over the last couple of decades the average amount harvested has increased from around five tonnes per day to ten tonnes per day. A team of occupational health researchers led by Fernanda Ludmilla Rossi Rocha dubbed this regime one of 'bio-psychological exhaustion'.[3] They found that the effects of the intense workload did not just lead to physical damage such as musculoskeletal pain, but also to emotional strain caused by the repetitive and risky work (accidents involving machete cuts and respiratory problems linked to dust and soot inhalation are commonplace). Thus, despite the widespread use of anti-inflammatory drugs and saline solutions to manage the daily shift, workers have tended not to last long in the job. At its worst, they have literally been worked to death. Despite health and safety legislation designed to protect agricultural workers, according to Luis Henrique Rafael, a lawyer with the state district attorney, between 2004 and 2008, at least eighteen cane cutters died in the state of São Paulo from dehydration, heart attacks or other ailments.[4]

In a sense, then, the working life of a cane cutter is condensed into a few years of extreme toil, at which point they have to be replaced by new workers willing to take on the challenge. This helps explain the prevalence of migrant workers in the sugar industry, as these are the people who most desperately seek waged employment and are most readily disciplined into the workforce. It also leads to the second strategy by which exploitation takes place: lowering the amount paid in wages.

One way this is achieved is through the use of bonded labour, where debt is used as a mechanism both to recruit workers and severely restrict their freedom, wages and bargaining power. Researching the experience of cane cutters in Tamil Nadu, India, the development scholar Isabelle Guérin found that, whereas most small-scale farmers relied on higher-paid local labour, those larger commercial farms run by separate managers relied on lower-paid migrant labour organized by the mill.[5] To do this, the mill used labour contractors based in low-caste communities who would recruit people through advance lump-sum payments before transporting them to the cane fields, often hundreds of kilometres from where they lived. In the face of widespread poverty and unemployment, these jobs are attractive to the workers as they provide a lump-sum loan that can be used to cover immediate expenditures – say, a marriage ceremony or medical fees – and offer a modicum of job security.

The story of Anand, a 34-year-old migrant worker from the village of Thondireddipalayam, is illustrative here. As reported by another researcher, Anand had been working as a cane cutter since the age of 16, travelling almost 1,000 km to work in the east of India some seasons. In 2007, Anand and his wife took an advance of 40,000 rupees (around £460) to help them buy a small plot of land near their village, left their children with their parents and began to work around their home state of Tamil Nadu for up to 11 months at a time. The researcher concluded that, because Anand was relatively close to his home village and could keep in contact via mobile phone, dependence on the labour contractor was reduced and abuse by them made less likely.[6]

However, what we do not find out is how long Anand and his wife had to work to pay off that debt, nor the quality of life they had whilst doing so. In her study, Guérin found that because of the pittance wage they received at the end of the season, most cane cutters did not pay off their debt immediately and so were trapped into returning year after year. Reliant on informal employment relationships that can readily evade legal requirements around labour rights, they also found themselves living in highly crowded and unhygienic makeshift camps with little recourse for complaint. In conclusion, then, Guérin argues that bonded labour is not something belonging only to the feudal age but that capitalist forms of (debt) bondage can emerge, which constitute 'unfree labour' or even, according to others, 'forced labour'. For our purposes, it is enough to note that, while slave-grown sugar may have been slowly abolished from the 1800s, there are still many other ways by which fundamental freedoms are curtailed in the industry today.

Another example of how wages are lowered is through child labour. Notoriously difficult to measure because it is purposely hidden from view, child labour has been reported in the sugar industries of at least twenty-three countries, including sugar-beet producers like Turkey where it is used to uproot the beets in harvesting operations not yet mechanized.[7] Across the world, it can be estimated that tens of thousands of children are incorporated into sugar's division of labour, assigned different work according to their age and sex. While older boys tend to do manual harvesting and chemical spraying, younger children are tasked with things like planting, weeding and stacking the crops for mechanical loading. For this, they are paid much less than adults, often because they are deemed to be 'family helpers' for which they do not need to be rewarded individually. A 2005 study in Guatemala found that some children were paid only 0.25 quetzals (around £0.02) per packet of cane sowed, while adults were paid 0.40 quetzals for exactly the same work. For the children, aged around 14 years old, this amounted to £3 wages for a full day's work – a clear breach of Guatemalan law.[8]

As well as working unpaid or underpaid on the site of *production*, children also work without recognition on the site of *reproduction*. This refers to domestic labour in the camps set up to accommodate migrant workers, where children – mainly girls – do chores such as cooking, washing clothes, and fetching water and wood. This mirrors much of the work done by children on family farms, which may not be directly related to sugar-cane production but is nonetheless invaluable to the farm's economic viability. In her study of small-scale sugar-cane farming in Fiji, the anthropologist Sue Carswell found that while children did contribute to the cultivation of sugar cane, they also tended vegetable gardens and subsistence plots, among other jobs.[9] Both of these unpaid forms of labour help to suppress wages by reducing the amount income-earners have to spend on subsistence.

Given the low wages, poor working conditions, family upheavals and general position of inferiority that many labourers endure, why do they carry on working in the sugar industry? As already mentioned, in some cases there is not a choice at all: individuals are trapped in relations of debt so must carry on working to try and pay it off. The paucity of alternative employment must also be considered. Sugar-cane migrants are drawn from poorer areas either inside the country (e.g. Northeast Brazil to Centre-South Brazil) or outside it (e.g. Burma to Thailand). This reflects the uneven spread of economic opportunities and continued absence of meaningful social security systems in many poor countries.

Another important draw is that, unlike much other farm work where remuneration is in kind or back-loaded, sugar-cane employers are more likely to pay in cash and on set dates. This type of remuneration is increasingly prized in rural areas because of the commodification of essential services. School fees, medical fees and water fees all require cash payment. The growing appeal of consumer goods, such as kitchen appliances and TVs, undoubtedly has a role to play too. The monetization of agrarian economies also brings with it moral complications. For example, a study in the Philippines found that many children were using their earnings from sugar-cane work to pay school fees – either for themselves or a sibling – meaning that efforts to eradicate child labour might have the unintended effect of forcing some children out of formal education.

But as important as the cash might be, even in those situations where a legal minimum wage is stipulated, it is usually insufficient to afford a decent standard of living. Table 4.1 compiles wage data for sugar-cane field workers taken from academic and civil society research. The sources are important since industry data tend to mask the lowest wages by providing company averages and/or ignoring the various tricks used to reduce wages below their stated levels, such as deliberately undercounting the amount of cane cut. What the table shows is that even when the legal minimum is paid, it still falls short of the recommended living wage.

We have concentrated thus far on the most abused groups of workers, but it should be recognized that the extensive division of labour has also stratified the working class, creating some positions with better pay, perks and working conditions. Some of these positions relate to

| Table 4.1 Wages for sugar-cane field workers, various years | | | |
|---|---|---|---|
| Region | Actual Wage | Minimum Wage | Living Wage | Source |
| Brazil (São Paulo) | BRL 25 per day (£7.50) | BRL 9.5 per day (£2.84) | BRL 44 per day (£13.17) | Mendonça et al. 2013[10] |
| Guatemala | GTQ 32 per day (£2.49) | GTQ 55 per day (£4.28) | GTQ 61 per day (£4.75) | COVERCO and International Labour Rights Fund 2005[11] |
| India (Tamil Nadu) | INR 80 per day (£0.90) | INR 80 per day (£0.90) | INR 250 per day (£2.81) | Guérin 2013[12] |
| Zambia | ZMK 772,200 per month (£91.19) | ZMK 700,000 per month (£82.66) | ZMK 1,060,000 per month (£125.18) | ActionAid 2013[13] |

*Note:* Living wage figures are taken from the Dutch organization WageIndicator Foundation and represent the minimum income needed for a one-person household to cover the cost of food, housing, transportation and other reasonable expenses at 2013 prices. The daily living wage was calculated by the author, based on someone working twenty days a month. Currencies converted at exchange rates on 1 January 2013.

the apparatus of control, such as managers and extension officers (often staffed by expatriates rather than nationals), while others relate to machine operation such as drivers, engineers, mechanics and technicians. This latter group are considered to be 'skilled' labourers and tend to be in a stronger bargaining position than their 'unskilled' counterparts – not just because of their relative scarcity in the labour market, but also because of their negotiating capacity.

Yet they can also be considered to be exploited in the sense that they produce far more output than they get rewarded for. An example here would be the driver of a mechanical harvester who does the work of one hundred manual harvesters but is not paid the equivalent of all their wages put together. Rather, after amortizing the costs of buying the machine, the extra value generated by the driver accrues to the company and is distributed by its managers, perhaps to owners in the form of dividends or themselves in higher salaries.

This method of exploitation might seem ethically preferable to the alternatives of increasing the workload or reducing the wage, and it has indeed been promoted by some of the younger and more cosmopolitan managerial class taking over the reins of the old plantation-style sugar companies. But it too is not without its problems. Most obviously, increasing labour productivity through the introduction of machinery and other types of technology typically leads to redundancies as fewer people are needed to produce the same amount of sugar. This can be offset to a degree by producing and selling more sugar, although, as we saw in the chapter on consumption, this cannot be done indefinitely even with the extra demand provided by biofuels.

Moreover, there is no guarantee that, just because a job becomes machine-based, it is also impervious to more abusive forms of exploitation. For example, the civil society group Repórter Brasil has highlighted cases where harvest, truck and tractor drivers were routinely working 24-hour shifts, leading in some instances to serious accidents due to exhaustion at the wheel.

Finally, efforts to increase labour productivity can also exacerbate gender inequalities. Again in Brazil, *IPS News* reported the story of Rosana do Carmo who was the only woman among a class of eighteen taking a tractor operation course and was ridiculed for taking on 'man's work' with jibes like 'your feet are too small for the pedals'.[14] Likewise, the sociologist Barbara Pini has documented the struggle of female drivers in the Australian sugar-cane industry to work within a masculine environment while also preserving their feminine identity.[15]

The general discrimination against women in the sugar industries deserves further discussion, as it is a phenomenon that can be identified throughout the labour hierarchy. Within farm work, their exclusion or underpayment is often naturalized with reference to their physical capacities, such as their feet being too small to work tractor pedals or their arms too weak to strike a machete. In my experience of visiting sugar-cane producers, women in the factories and administrative buildings also occupied low-ranking positions such as cleaners and secretaries, which again corresponds with cultural stereotypes about 'women's work'.

These fallacies about what women are capable of doing are exposed by those many examples where, given the chance to work alongside men, they often exceed average labour productivity, even in tasks like cane cutting.[16] Yet, even in those instances where there *are* greater proportions of female field workers, it is rarely a triumph for gender equality. In her study of the Pelwate Sugar Corporation in Sri Lanka, the anthropologist Nandini Gunewardena found that (male) managers said they preferred to recruit women because of their dutiful and hard-working character – note the naturalization of difference again – when in reality it was because they were easier to coerce.[17] Not coincidentally, managers at the company had previously been confronted by hostile male workers armed with machetes, complaining about unequal wages.

As well as denying women equal earnings, this asymmetry also spills over into other areas of the economy. For example, prostitution is common in many sugar towns (especially where seasonal workers leave their wives behind when they migrate), leading to increases in sexually transmitted diseases among other dangers. Women's economic dependence on the larger wage package earned by men can also feed into social discourse that portrays them as needy and powerless, becoming something of a self-reinforcing cycle. Even at the very highest level, sugar remains a man's world. At the 2013 International Sugar Organization conference, which brought together more than 400 executives and senior managers from around the world, just 16 per cent were female.[18] It is a topic worthy of further research as to whether this masculine bias spills over into our everyday language, too, with terms like 'sugar daddy' and 'sweet talker' typically being used to describe male command over the female body.

*Farming for the financier*
In thinking about the labour process, landowning farmers are a difficult category to analyse. On the one hand, they own part of the means of production (the farmland) and are often bosses themselves, employing field workers to help them plant, cultivate and harvest the crops. Yet, on the other hand, they can also be extremely dependent on the mill or processor buying their crops, such that they become little more than propertied labourers themselves. Although they retain juridical ownership of the farmland, what happens on it is effectively controlled by industrial capital. In some cases, as we shall see in the next chapter on land, milling and processing companies do buy land themselves, cutting farmers out of the production process completely and proletarianizing all forms of labour. However, there are also countervailing forces to be taken into consideration: legal conventions might prevent mills and processors from acquiring land; political conditions might require them to keep farmers in business; and economic calculations might show that it is more profitable to pass some of the agricultural risks onto others.

As with waged labour, there is a hierarchy of farmers and this tends to map onto the size of their farms. Some farmers own large tracts of land and machinery, too, although the latter may require credit and/or co-ownership to acquire (a 12-row sugar-beet harvester called Hexx Traxx was released in the United Kingdom last year with a whopping price tag of £500,000). Other farmers, meanwhile, own only small plots of land that may be poorly irrigated and difficult to access to boot. Unsurprisingly, it is the small-scale farmers that are most at risk in the sugar industry.

In India, there are millions of small-scale sugar-cane farmers and, just as with migrant workers in the country, indebtedness is a major problem. Money has to be borrowed for upfront costs like fertilizer and cannot always be paid back, especially in years when the price offered by the mill is low or payments are delayed. According to the charity Christian Aid, this is common among many cash-crop farmers in India, due to a steep rise in the costs of inputs, particularly as government fertilizer subsidies have fallen away, and a lack of access to cheap credit as banks pursue a more commercial mandate.[19]

At its most acute, indebtedness has led to violent protests and even suicide. In Uttar Pradesh in 2013, the day after sugar-cane farmer Satyapal Singh hanged himself because he could not repay his 200,000 rupee debt (around £2,000), two hundred farmers stormed into the compound of the local sugar mill to protest about cane arrears. Later that year, the federal agriculture minister Sharad Pawar announced a range of measures to address the agrarian crisis engulfing the sector as a whole. One was the export subsidy noted in the last chapter; another was state-subsidized loans and debt relief for the mills, which were then put under strict orders to pass this onto farmers. However, such sticking-plasters are unlikely to prevent farmers falling back into unsustainable debt, and official suicide figures do suggest this is a recurring problem. At least 270,000 farmers in India alone – mainly those growing cotton, coffee, sugar cane and other cash crops – killed themselves between 1995 and 2013.

In contrast to the Indian case, in which farmers have largely borrowed money from banks or farm societies to pay for their running costs, in Kenya the mill itself has assumed the role of financier. In a 2014 story published in the Kenyan newspaper *The Daily Nation*, the country's biggest milling group, Mumias Sugar Company, was accused of charging excessive prices for inputs and services and applying exorbitant rates of interest to them.[20] Numerous farmers interviewed said that, as a result, instead of taking away a pay cheque at the end of the season, they were handed notes saying that they owed the mill money.

Not all cases of sugar-cane farming end in ruin, of course. In Swaziland, the 1,200 farmers that entered the sugar industry during the late 2000s, funded in large part by EU grants, have generally done well. Alongside a small profit on selling sugar cane, they also benefited from access to irrigated water that could be used for subsistence crop production, and in some cases did farm work and paid themselves a wage. Yet this too is a cautionary tale. Since the 1990s, more than a thousand small-scale farmers have been encouraged to enter the sugar industry by the government and millers but have had to finance themselves by borrowing money at commercial rates. Even after the anticipated seven-year repayment period had passed, many of these farmers were still paying off their debts and had little profit to speak of, leading to severe hardship and tensions within the community over the fallout from their mortgaged future.

In economic terms, the perpetuation of debt in sugar-cane and sugar-beet farming can be seen to result from high and upfront costs combined with low and untimely revenue. The latter part of this equation is structured by the fact that the mill/processor is usually a monopsonist, meaning that it is the sole buyer of cane/beet and is therefore in a strong position to dictate terms and essentially bargain away the surplus value generated by the growing of the crop. If farmers do not like these terms, there is rarely an alternative customer to whom they can sell their crops.

This dependence manifests itself in all sorts of industry politics. Negotiations over the price of crops for that season are often highly charged affairs, requiring politicians to intervene, as regularly happens in India. Even the way that mills determine the quality of crops can spark conflict. In Belize in 2009, cane farmers reacted with hostility to the introduction of equipment that would sample the sucrose content of the cane they delivered to the mill and which they believed would lower the prices they were paid. In the ensuing protests, one farmer, Atanacio Gutierrez, was shot dead and others injured in clashes with police.

But as well as being antagonistic, the mutual dependence of farmers and millers/processors can also result in collective endeavours, especially when the interests of the national industry as a whole are threatened. Thus in the United States, family farmers growing sugar beet and sugar cane have often acted as de facto lobbyists, making trips to Washington, DC to ward off threats to existing sugar policy. Collin Peterson, the leading Democrat in the federal Agricultural Committee, has openly noted their importance: 'These guys are disciplined, they know the arguments, and they are organized.'[21]

In sum, because of debt or other forms of economic dependence, as well as more benign reasons such as a desire to stay on the land and preserve a long-standing way of life, farmers can find themselves locked into the sugar business. Together with the factors identified in the first section, this helps explain the stark generational juxtaposition that exists on many sugar farms today: old farmers directing young workers, with neither making much money out of it.

## Modernization and mass redundancy

For many reformers, the correct response to the developmental challenges facing farmers and workers is for the sugar industry to 'modernize'. There is no fixed meaning to this term: in colonial South-East Asia in the 1880s, it rested on the introduction of cane breeding and central sugar mills, in 1960s post-revolutionary Cuba on the adoption of agricultural machinery and collective farm ownership. Today, the technological and organizational change of modernization is associated primarily with mechanized harvesting, precision farming and factory diversification, which typically involves increasing both the capital intensity of production and its scale. For advocates of modernization, gangs of manual field workers and patchworks of small-scale farmers are the epitome of rural backwardness, bound to suffer one way or another.

Yet as noted in the previous discussion on labour productivity, such modernization also results in redundancy. Or in Marxist terms, dead labour embodied in the machine progressively replaces living labour. The trend is not unique to sugar. As the rural sociologist Ben White has noted, with the possible exception of floriculture, all commercial agrifood production today is labour expelling.[22]

The idea that modernization will assist labour, then, is a contradictory one since in its current form it essentially involves destroying large numbers of jobs. The awkwardness of this fact is perhaps reflected in the paucity of sugar-industry employment data. One can easily find statistics on crop yields or fertilizer application, but transparent and reliable employment figures are far more elusive! Table 4.2 gathers together some disparate sources and shows two important things. First, in every region of the world thousands of people are losing their jobs. Second, this is even happening in some places where output is increasing. Put simply, the picture is one of more sugar, less labour.

It is also the poorest among the workforce who are most at risk of redundancy. In São Paulo state, for example, sugar-cane field workers have been hardest hit. Across the same period cited in Table 4.2, almost 50 per cent of this low-wage occupational group lost their jobs, amounting to more than 84,000 people. Likewise, in the United States, and again across the same period cited in the table, most of the farms that disappeared were small and mid-sized landholdings, while the number of farms of more than 2,000 acres (three square miles!) actually increased. This is one reason why the common refrain in American political circles that farm jobs will be put at risk if US sugar policy is liberalized rings hollow: they are at risk anyway.

Technological unemployment does of course create some work elsewhere. The US-based machinery manufacturer John Deere, Brazilian-based engineer Oderbrecht, South African-based consultant Booker Tate and Chinese-based constructor China National Complete Plant Import & Export Corporation have all become leading suppliers of goods and services to the global sugar industry, benefiting from its heavy investment in capital-intensive production processes. Another South African company, Airborne, has even touted its use of unmanned drones to fly over

Table 4.2 Levels of redundancy in different sugar-producing regions, various years

| Region | Sector | Time period | Percentage change in output | Percentage change in employment | Absolute change in employment | Source |
|---|---|---|---|---|---|---|
| Brazil (São Paulo) | Cane growing and milling | 2007–2013 | +9.5 per cent tonnes cane harvested | −5.8 per cent total employment | −18,440 people | Brazilian Ministry of Work and Employment 2014[23] |
| EU 25 | Beet farming and processing | 2003–2013 | −9.8 per cent tonnes beet harvested | −42.9 per cent farmers and factory workers | −130,972 farmers and factory workers | European Committee of Sugar Manufacturers 2014[24] |
| Southern Africa (Illovo Sugar Company) | Cane growing and milling | 2009–2014 | +1.6 per cent tonnes sugar produced | −25.2 per cent permanent and seasonal company employees | −10,457 permanent and seasonal company employees | Illovo Sugar 2014[25] |
| USA | Cane and beet farming | 2002–2007 | −10.4 per cent acres farmed | −21.2 per cent farmers | −1,266 farmers | USDA 2014[26] |

sugar-cane fields and spray chemicals in areas where pests or diseases are detected.

In all these cases, the expansionary thrust is targeted at areas with lower than average labour productivity. The economist Beate Zimmermann calculated in 2002 that labourers in Australia produced ten times as much sugar per hour worked than those in India.[27] Unsurprisingly, India is one of the countries being actively targeted by John Deere among others. Yet the overall result as far as labour is concerned is a net loss of jobs in sugar, concentrated among poorer farmers and workers.

What happens to the people displaced from sugar production? Experts of a neo-liberal persuasion have argued that they should quickly be absorbed by another industry, probably in the urban service sector, given its relatively fast growth rate in most economies of the world. In practice, however, most of the newly unemployed have drifted, left to do odd jobs in the informal economy, to migrate to shanty towns in search of work, or to take early retirement and live as family dependants.

For example, in 2005 in the midst of EU reform, the World Bank economist Donald Mitchell argued that, rather than fight the reform process, most countries in the Caribbean should simply abandon the crop and instead 'devote resources to retraining workers and developing sugar lands into commercial, residential and agricultural uses'.[28] What transpired in Trinidad, where this advice was ultimately followed, was that those workers who had initially got jobs in construction saw the temporary work dry up following recession, while those assigned plots of land to farm were still waiting for them to be disbursed years after they had been taken out of cane production.

It was a familiar story across the Caribbean: rural workers and small farmers struggled to find stable employment, while investors seemed effortlessly to acquire former sugar-cane land for golf courses and hotel complexes. To be sure, the situation differs depending on its context. Beet farmers in the United Kingdom forced out of business by EU reform turned to other, less profitable crops like oilseed rape to provide alternative income, criticizing the short notice and scant compensation given by British Sugar in the process.[29] Meanwhile, field workers in São Paulo have been sent on industry-sponsored retraining programmes, although difficulties have become apparent in making this accessible to all workers (especially women and those with less schooling) and in guaranteeing jobs at the end, since only a small proportion can be reabsorbed by the modernizing sugar industry.

*Labour organization*
Workers and farmers have not been passive about the way the sugar-cane and sugar-beet industries have been run, organizing themselves in various ways so as to advance their collective interests. Indeed, some of the earliest sugar-based trade unions have since turned into established political parties, including the Jamaica Labour Party, the Mauritius Labour Party and the American Popular Revolutionary Alliance in Peru.

One reason why the sugar industry became such a potent source of trade union activism was precisely the factory system outlined earlier. Bringing together workers under one central authority focused their powers of resistance, especially those within the mill who were also physically concentrated under one roof. This was certainly the case in South Africa, where the first independent union for black workers in the whole of Natal was formed in 1980 as a result of wildcat strikes by mill workers who downed tools and brought sugar production to a halt. Despite the splintered nature of the labour movement that followed – some becoming populist and supporting anti-Apartheid demands, some remaining 'workerist' and focusing on shop-floor concerns – trade unionism has remained an integral means by which labourers have levied demands in the country. In 2014, three unions representing 5,500 workers went on strike, causing the first industry stoppage in seventeen years and leading to a state-negotiated settlement for wage increases of up to 10 per cent. In other countries the state has not been so bipartisan. That same year in neighbouring Swaziland, where multi-party elections are banned and the unions are the de facto political opposition, police forces fired tear gas and water at workers striking outside the Illovo sugar mill.

Farmers, too, have unionized. In the United Kingdom, they have been represented by the National Farmers Union, which has engaged in annual negotiations with British Sugar (Illovo's sister company) over the crop price. While these negotiations have not reached the level of radicalism seen in southern Africa, beet farmers have openly acknowledged their need to club together against British Sugar, given its monopsony power, and they have lobbied in the EU to make sure their right to collective negotiation would not be dissolved as part of the reform of the Common Agricultural Policy.

A more vociferous and populist farmer activism can be found in the Bharatiya Kisan Union of India, which has challenged wider social inequality between what they portray as downtrodden rural peasants and corrupt urban elites. Their demands for higher prices and cheaper inputs for cash crops like sugar cane and wheat have been advanced through tactics such as roadblocks, sit-downs and local assemblies, directed primarily at those in political office rather than at company managers. Yet the Bharatiya

Kisan Union also shows how unions can fail to live up to their moral claim to solidarity. The geographer Craig Jeffrey noted how the middle-caste richer peasants that ran the organization were not above low-level corruption themselves, ingratiating themselves with officials in the Cane Societies in order to get better quota supply rights to the detriment of lower-caste and lower-class farmers.

But arguably the biggest barrier to unions acting effectively is their continued *dis*organization by the state. Since 2000, the International Labour Organization has investigated complaints about the violation of freedom of association in sugar industries in twenty-five different countries. These have been as diverse as Argentina, Guatemala, Indonesia, Iran, Mauritius and Ukraine. One of the most egregious cases has been in Fiji. Following the military coup in 2006, workers at the Fiji Sugar Corporation saw their trade union put under increasing pressure. Having already declared a State of Emergency and suspended many civil rights (a journalist was detained in 2011 simply for reporting on a sugar mill's maintenance problems), the government also refused to enter into any negotiations with workers and sent in army personnel to 'observe' trade union strike ballots.

Another common form of labour organization is the cooperative, in which workers and farmers take on collective ownership duties. For example, in Germany, the biggest shareholder of Südzucker is the South German Sugar Beet Processing Cooperative, whose members receive a dividend on the company's profit in addition to the payment for beet deliveries.[30] France's biggest producer, Tereos, is completely owned by cooperatives, which together comprise 12,000 sugar-beet farmers. While these seem a benign alternative to the corporation, a note of caution must be sounded. In Tereos's case, as the company has internationalized and greater levels of autonomy have been transferred to its executive management, questions have been raised about how much direction it still takes from growers and their elected representatives on the board of directors. Moreover, the cooperative structure is unevenly applied, not being extended to those famers supplying the foreign subsidiaries that Tereos has acquired.

The question of whose interests are represented in the cooperative is also pertinent in the case of India. In the country's biggest sugar-producing state of Maharashtra, most mills are cooperatively owned. This is a legacy of the efforts of Vitthalrao Vikhe Patil, who in 1948 organized the sugar-cane growers of forty-four villages to acquire their own mill, and, later, of the then Bombay state government which supported other cooperative ventures. The average membership of sugar-cane cooperatives today is around 20,000 farmers, the idea being that the cooperative provides them with inputs and credit as well as their communities with educational, medical and religious facilities. Yet a team of economists led by Abhijit Banerjee found that more money was being spent by the cooperatives on community projects and other construction works than on providing farmers with higher cane prices. The reason for this, they concluded, was that a handful of richer farmers had the time, money and connections needed to get elected as cooperative directors and, once in power, sought to reward themselves by allocating business contracts to family and friends, at the same time as accruing greater political prestige from the commissioning of big projects.

The relationship between cooperatives and trade unions can also be fraught, reflecting the tensions that exist between the farming and wage-earning factions of labour. In the United States, the cooperative structure of beet farmers is often cited as evidence that the sugar industry is run for the benefit of rural communities. This was betrayed by the strike in 2011 by 1,300 factory workers at the American Crystal Sugar processing plant, owned by the Red River Valley Sugarbeet Growers Association. Lasting for more than twenty months, during which time union members were locked out and replacement workers hired to keep the factory running, the union finally accepted the deal of wage increases in exchange for cuts to health benefits and increased use of contract jobs.

In other instances, unions have been displaced rather than defeated by cooperatives. In Colombia in the late 1990s, the law was changed so that field workers had to organize themselves into 'associated labour cooperatives' and complete the tasks they were assigned under their own stewardship. While this may sound empowering, in practice this meant that because they were now considered to be their own bosses, their real employers were no longer obliged to pay social security benefits nor enter into collective wage bargaining. Commenting at the time, Senator Jorge Enrique Robledo said 'the *raison d'être* of these cooperatives is simply to bring down the price of labour'.[31]

A final institutional form into which labour movements have crystallized is the state-owned company. This is a more top-down form of ownership than the voluntary cooperative and reached its apogee in the 1970s when sugar assets were nationalized in Belize, Guyana, Jamaica, Peru and Trinidad among other countries. This reflected the influence of socialist political parties and the thinking of the 'New World' group of Caribbean intellectuals who depicted the plantations as parasitic legacies of colonialism. The wave of nationalization also echoed earlier calls made during the independence movement for workers to regain their humanity by engaging in collective struggle and renouncing the debilitating identities of (Afro-Caribbean) 'nigger' and (Indo-Caribbean) 'coolie' that had also been inherited from the European empire.

However, the ideological pendulum has since swung away from public ownership and towards private ownership. There have been various justifications for this. Neo-liberals have criticized the inflexibility of state-owned sugar companies to engage in restructuring initiatives, even when the very survival of the industry seems to depend upon it. Others have cast doubt on the motives of public ownership, which have been linked to enriching elites, eliminating domestic opposition and demonizing traditionally wealthy groups, rather than being genuine attempts to democratize the economy. The only recent cases of sugar nationalization, in Sri Lanka (2011) and Venezuela (2008–2010), have done little to allay such concerns.

This is not to say that privatization is somehow apolitical. In Uttar Pradesh, for example, investigations by public auditors found that mills which were taken into state ownership in the 1970s to protect farmers against insolvency (and now being privatized for the very same reason!) were sold off on the cheap in the 2010s to businessmen with close ties to influential political parties. Meanwhile, in Turkey, the privatization of some state-owned beet processors in the early 2000s, along with the elimination of price controls and the liberalization of trade, took place largely at the behest of the World Bank, which had lent the country US$600 million to roll out its Agricultural Reform Implementation Project. Hardly a triumph for national democracy. Indeed, plans to privatize the remaining state-owned sugar processors in 2010 were put on hold by the courts following widespread protests against the government's general privatization agenda.

## Governing labour

As in other sectors of the economy, workers and farmers involved in sugar production should be subject to the general labour laws and policies put in place by the state (although, as we have noted, these are not always implemented). Still, national regulations on things like minimum wage and bargaining rights have provided an important political and legal standpoint around which labour practices are structured and so are important to monitor, even when focusing on specific industries.

A recent example was the decision by the Bolivian government in 2014 to effectively legalize child labour, abrogating its commitment to the ILO's Minimum Age Convention and allowing children aged 12–14 to undertake contract work on the proviso that they do not work more than six hours a day. In Bolivia, child labour is extensive, including in sugar-cane agriculture. The argument put forward by supporters of this legislation, including some children in the Union of Child and Adolescent Workers, is that at least now they will enjoy the same rights as adult workers and be able to better provide for their families. Opponents have argued that these rights are unlikely to be enforced and that the new law ultimately undermines progress towards fair wages for adults and better schooling for children.

The state has also made more specific interventions on behalf of capitalists involved in sugar production, exempting them from general labour laws or accommodating them with new ones. A famous example in the United States is the 'H-2' immigration programme, which allowed foreign workers to enter the country on temporary visas and thereby overcome the difficulties that sugar and other agricultural industries had in finding abundant cheap labour at harvest time. In Florida, this was used to 'import' thousands of cane cutters from the Caribbean every year, a practice which persisted until the 1990s when the Jamaican migrant Bernard Bygrave questioned his pay packet with a local attorney and the resultant class-action lawsuit exposed endemic underpayment of wages by all five major sugar-cane companies in the state. While the lawsuit did not oppose the H-2 programme itself, paradoxically it had the effect of convincing the companies involved that manual cane cutters would only become more expensive, therefore hastening their shift to agricultural mechanization which removed the need for migrant labour in the first place.[32]

H-2 migrants are still working in the American sugar industry, albeit in fewer numbers and coming from Latin America rather than the Caribbean. Application forms downloaded from the US Department of Labor Public Registry show Louisiana to be the most common destination, with workers hired to operate farm machinery and plant cane for US$9.50–US$10.00 an hour. It is worth noting that sugar-cane and sugar-beet employers in the United States, along with those in cotton ginning, are also exempt from laws on overtime payments and maximum working hours (up to a period of fourteen weeks) applied to American as well as non-American workers.[33]

A similar case of migrant exploitation exists in the Dominican Republic, although here the Dominican state has assisted more by turning a blind eye and allowing labour governance to pass into the hands of sugar companies. For the Dominican Republic, the labour frontier has long been located in its impoverished neighbour Haiti and, during the dictatorship of the Duvalier family (1957–1986), it was the Haitian government that orchestrated the migration of its people to the Dominican plantations, for which the Duvalier regime was richly rewarded. After their overthrow, illegal recruitment filled the gap. This was led by a network of labour contractors who collaborated with border officials and transport agents to bring busloads of undocumented Haitians into the rural Dominican shanty towns, known as *bateyes*, where they would work for state-owned and privately owned companies.

The fate of these workers was brought to international attention by the controversial 2008 film *The Price of Sugar*, which followed the efforts of the priest Father Christopher Hartley to mobilize the brutalized sugar-cane workers of the *bateyes*. The film was a deliberate attempt to use the United States' preferential trade allowance to the Dominican Republic as political leverage. Not only did it frequently mention the subsidies given by American consumers to sugar suppliers in the Dominican Republic, but it was also used by the director Bill Haney and 'star' Christopher Hartley in their subsequent political activism, even being screened during a meeting with the US Congressional Human Rights Caucus. Needless to say, the company at the centre of the allegations, the Vicini Group, was not best pleased. It sued the director for factual inaccuracy and tried to suppress screenings of the film. Hinting at the close ties that still remain between the state and the sugar industry (despite its privatization in the late 1990s), even the Dominican foreign minister waded into the debate, calling the film part of a 'campaign of hate' against the industry. But Hartley continued his crusade, and following his complaint under the clauses of the United States' free trade agreement with the Dominican Republic, the US Department of Labor undertook its own investigation. Released in 2013, this found numerous violations of labour law, as well as flaws in the labour inspection process, such as failing to interview workers properly.

Although the Dominican government has been slow to implement US recommendations in the sugar sector, in

2014, and under considerable pressure from social justice groups, they did relent on the more high-profile issue of human rights for Dominican-born children of Haitian migrants. Many of these 'stateless' people are descendants of sugar workers still living in the *bateyes* and have long been denied citizenship or even residence status. By allowing them to apply for identification cards and even naturalization, this opened the door to legal employment beyond the plantation – a pressing issue, given that only 15,000 of the estimated 400,000 stateless Haitian descendants living in the Dominican Republic today are employed as seasonal sugar labour. At the time of writing, though, the take-up of these regularization options has been low, a fact that interior minister José Ramón Fadul attributed to the refusal of Dominican-based employers to provide certificates of employment where required.[34]

While the state has frequently acted to support capital accumulation in sugar production, there have also been moments when it has been cajoled and coerced into defending labour. The case of Brazil is a good example of this seeming schizophrenia. Whilst bearing witness to the intensification of manual labour, the state has also managed to significantly reduce the number of people working in the most abusive 'slave-like' conditions in the sugar-cane industry – more than 10,000 being 'liberated' from their workplace between 2003 and 2011.[35] This has been attributed to the determination of inspectors in the Ministry of Labour and Employment to investigate rural employers and the legal powers held by the Labour Prosecutors' Office to prevent companies subcontracting core tasks, like harvesting, and holding them criminally responsible for any breaches of labour law.

Alongside this, novel policy instruments launched by the government have created economic incentives to tackle labour abuses. The most important has been the 'National Pact to Eradicate Slave Labour', in which major retailers and banks made public commitments not to buy products or lend money to companies published on the Ministry of Labour and Employment's 'Dirty List' of firms convicted of slave labour. Civil society organizations like Repórter Brasil were also involved and helped identify likely sources of labour rights violations and the supply chains that were affected.

This system of governance, in which private-sector actors would police themselves, was not without its critics. Some questioned its impartiality when the sugar miller Cosan sought a court injunction to get itself off the list just days after the Brazilian state bank had said it would suspend financing to the company and Wal-Mart planned to suspend purchases of its packaged sugar. Nevertheless, the Dirty List made sufficient advances to encourage the Brazilian government to attempt another voluntary initiative based on 'name and shame' reporting, this time to provide better-quality work. The 'National Commitment to Enhance Working Conditions in Sugarcane' was launched in 2009 and involved independent auditors visiting sugarcane producers and awarding them a social certificate if they met certain criteria, such as providing personal protective equipment. However, this quickly became apparent as a rubber-stamping exercise – the Public Prosecutor's Office later found some of the certificates had been awarded on the basis of poor-quality, or even falsified, audits – and despite the initial enthusiasm from government, when the first of the four-year certificates began to expire in 2013 the programme was not renewed.

Without legal enforcement, the scrutiny of civil society organizations or clear commercial incentives for receipt of the social certificates, voluntary initiatives like the National

Commitment relied solely on progressive ideals to stir managers into effecting change. In this context, and given the imperatives of profit making, it was perhaps inevitable that the initiative would do little on its own to drive labour standards upwards.

## Conclusion

A variety of incentives have encouraged managers to discipline labour and appropriate as much value from it as they can. Chief among these has been the imperative to accumulate wealth, spurred by threats of market competition and capital divestment should they slacken in this quest. This is one reason why international trade liberalization is so important: it is one of the most immediate ways of increasing competition and intensifying scrutiny on production costs like wages. Strategies to bolster labour productivity have included increasing the workload, decreasing the wage and introducing new technologies and organizational forms. In other cases, surplus value has been bargained away from farmers by banks, millers and landowners through different forms of market power. Each of these has had quite different effects, but it is notable that all tend to take advantage of established hierarchies of inequality – be it racialized inequalities that treat migrants as subhuman 'Others', gendered inequalities that discriminate against those doing 'women's work', or class inequalities that pass on borrowing risk to small-scale family farmers. They also combine to produce the treadmill effect, whereby labourers are left running to stand still: farmers increase their yields, and workers put in longer shifts, but both remain in a precarious financial position.

We also saw how the politics of sugar-industry labour extended far beyond the site of production. Reliance on unpaid domestic labour to help workers cope with the strains of the job, manipulation of the job market to assure ready supplies of 'flexible' workers and the repression of organized labour as collective economic agents have all benefited employers. Yet, thanks to the efforts of labourers themselves, usually in conjunction with those in sympathetic state institutions, some of the more egregious tools of exploitation have been blunted. One way of achieving this has been for unions to co-opt themselves into technological projects designed to enhance labour productivity on the proviso that the financial benefits are equally shared. But to the extent that this form of modernization has been based on saving labour costs rather than valorizing labour output, unions have also had to accept the expulsion of poorer workers and smaller farmers from the industry.

At the same time, though, there is also a sting in the tail for capital. The steady exodus of workers from the industry has weakened the political power that sugar companies have historically had as vital rural employers. To recapture this influence, they have begun to cast themselves instead as crucial cogs in the green economy – a transformation we explore in the next chapter.

CHAPTER FIVE

# Expanding and Exhausting Land

The last chapter highlighted the issue of labour redundancy in the global sugar industry. In one sense, the issues surrounding land are rather different. Here, the recent dynamic has been one of expansion rather than expulsion, at least as far as sugar-cane production is concerned. As Figure 5.1 shows, 31 million hectares of land worldwide were dedicated to growing sugar crops in 2013, an area bigger than the entire United Kingdom. Most of the growth in planting has been in Brazil, where during the last decade more land was converted to sugar cane than in all the other countries of the world combined. While the amount of land planted with sugar beet has fallen – the biggest decline taking place in Eastern Europe – the sugar-cane booms in Brazil, and to a lesser extent in India, China, Thailand and Pakistan, have more than offset this.

The increased rate of expansion experienced since the mid-2000s has been common to many of the fungible crops used to produce food, feed and biofuel. Collectively, it has been labelled by critics a 'global land grab', likened to the scramble for Africa and other territorial conquests that were part of European colonialism. A major difference, of course, is that during the colonial era investors went in search of cheap land *and* cheap labour, whereas now only the former is needed in great supply. But there is also a continuity to explore, both with the colonial past and with the previous chapter on labour. This centres on the exploitation

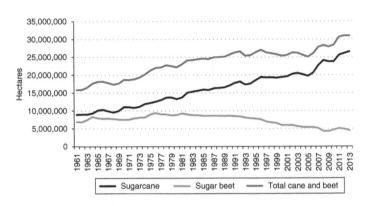

Figure 5.1 Worldwide area planted to sugar crops, 1961–2013
*Source*: FAOSTAT

of land and its gradual exhaustion as a productive resource. The management of this dynamic has become crucial to the industry's claim to provide green energy and sustainable agriculture, a claim that, on closer inspection, must be contested.

## The global land grab

In the same way that food aid was politicized by renaming it 'food dumping', the large-scale and long-term land acquisitions that have characterized the recent wave of property rights transfers have been dubbed by some 'land grabbing'. What these critics have sought to disturb is the win–win rhetoric that surrounds such deals, whereby investors are said to win as they expand their business and host countries to win as they boost growth, jobs and tax collection. For those who have studied the patterns of agrarian change which follow such investments, these narratives deliberately obfuscate the existence of losers: typically existing land-users, including peasant farmers, forest dwellers, indigenous communities and landless workers. These groups have rarely had a say in whether the land is converted to cash-crop production, have rarely got fair compensation if it is and have regularly been opposed if they protest against their sudden dislocation.

Critics have also been keen to point out that land grabs have done little to help reduce domestic levels of hunger. The International Land Coalition reported that between 2000 and 2010 there were deals concluded or under negotiation for 203 million hectares of land, largely in the Global South. Of those that could be verified, 58 per cent were for biofuel production and just 17 per cent for food production, much of which was produced for export.[1]

In Brazil, the effects of sugar-cane expansion have been widely felt. In São Paulo state, the centre of sugar-cane production, rural land prices increased by 57 per cent between 2005 and 2011. Whilst this provided a windfall to landowners, it also pushed out other agricultural activities and precluded government efforts to acquire land for the settlement of indigenous people. In fact, indigenous people have been punished twice over as the sugar-cane frontier has since moved into states beyond São Paulo and encroached on their ancestral land. One prominent case highlighted by Survival International, an organization dedicated to the self-determination of tribal peoples, involved the US-based agribusiness Bunge and one of its customers, Coca-Cola. Bunge was accused of buying sugar cane that had been grown on land being used by Guaraní Indians, since the Guaraní had been unable to claim legal ownership of their land as the state programme to demarcate indigenous territories had ground to a halt. In the meantime, cane planting had encroached and led to pesticides from planes being sprayed over their communities and fresh water and fishing rivers being contaminated.

Such encounters have generated violent confrontation. In 2012 alone, the Brazil-based Indigenous Missionary Council reported 396 land conflicts in sugar cane-growing regions. These were typically linked to the forced removal of encampments that the displaced tribespeople had set up along roadsides or on the fringes of cane farms. A more insidious violence is caused by the psychological effects of living in overcrowded and unfamiliar conditions: that same year, suicide rates among the Guaraní had climbed to more than thirty times the national average.[2]

As well as the effects directly attributable to sugar-cane expansion, there have also been indirect effects. One of the most controversial of these has been the consequences of sugar-cane producers buying up land used by cattle ranchers and dairy farmers, and whether this has led the latter to clear more land for grazing by deforesting protected ecological sites. In their assessment, the World Bank concluded that, although the productivity gains in sugar-cane and livestock production had mitigated most of this effect, 'the resulting higher price of land has probably put pressure on pasture expansion further north to the Cerrado and the Amazon biome'.[3]

One of the unforeseen consequences of Amazonian deforestation for the sugar-cane industry has been the intensification of droughts that have withered the crops of São Paulo some one thousand kilometres away. Brazilian meteorologists have argued that the 'flying rivers' of water vapour that evaporate from the Amazon forest and deposit rain in the south of the country have become more infrequent, threatening the hydrological pump that keeps Brazil from massive desertification. We return to the incidence of such ecological feedback effects later in the chapter.

Alongside changes in the extensity of land under sugar cane, there have also been changes in its ownership. No longer is it the traditional plantation families who own most of the sugar-cane land in Brazil but the millers and, through them, a host of multinational companies and stock market investors. Including the portion that they lease out to tenant farmers, the International Sugar Organization has estimated that sugar-cane mills now own around 75 per cent of the land under cane in the country.[4]

This acquisition of land by industrial capital has had two strategic dimensions. First, it has dissolved the distinction between landowner and producer. This cuts out the need for them to pay for both rent and crop deliveries, and, given that landlords could readily use their assets for other ends, also allows the mills to exert greater control over the production process (continuing the 'factory farming' theme from the previous chapter). The second reason they have bought land is to treat it as an asset in its own right, deepening its commodification. Several sugar-cane companies have even spun out property arms. In 2008, Cosan launched a company called Radar, which, together with equity investment from US-based pension funds, invested the equivalent of £380 million pounds in Brazilian land that it has since leased out for sugar-cane, soybean, corn and cotton farming. Other companies have moved beyond agriculture altogether. In South Africa, the sugar company Tongaat Hulett has built residential and office complexes in salubrious urban environments, advertised as 'luxurious gated communities . . . that have come to symbolise upmarket living'.[5]

The biggest increase of sugar-cane planting in absolute terms has been in Brazil. But, as shown in Table 5.1, it has also grown rapidly in relative terms in countries like Cambodia, Laos, Paraguay and Zambia. The social impacts have been just as severe here, if not more so.

In Cambodia, the recent expansion was based on three

Table 5.1  Biggest proportional increases in sugar-cane planting, 2003–2013

| Country | 2003 hectares | 2013 hectares | Absolute increase hectares | Percentage increase |
|---------|---------------|---------------|----------------------------|---------------------|
| Cambodia | 8,482 | 28,500 | 20,018 | 236 per cent |
| Laos | 8,962 | 21,000 | 12,038 | 134 per cent |
| Paraguay | 62,205 | 116,000 | 53,795 | 86 per cent |
| Brazil | 5,371,020 | 9,835,169 | 4,464,149 | 83 per cent |
| Zambia | 22,000 | 39,000 | 17,000 | 77 per cent |

*Note*: Excludes countries with 2013 sugar-cane areas under 10,000 hectares.

*Source*: FAOSTAT.

sets of land concessions granted by the government to a constellation of investors led by ruling party Senator Ly Yong Phat and the Thai-based milling groups Mitr Phol and Khon Kaen Sugar. These concessions took advantage of the fact that the vast majority of rural communities did not have legal title to their land, a legacy of the Khmer Rouge regime which banned private property and burned people's land records. Legal procedures designed to protect citizens were also flouted by the Cambodian state. Petitions to authorities to prevent the transfer of land were ignored and the compensation provided in the form of finance or land was either inadequate or simply non-existent. Those who resisted dispossession and tried to remain in their homes were forcibly removed by police and military security forces, with buildings burned, land bulldozed and animals shot to make the point clear.

The human rights group FIAN estimate that, in total, more than 1,700 families lost land that was being used to grow rice, raise livestock and source clean water and firewood.[6] With grim irony, the sugar produced on the concessions has ended up being exported to the EU under its

Everything But Arms agreement, the free trade deal mentioned in chapter 3 which was intended to help the world's poorest people 'trade their way out of poverty'.[7]

In media coverage of large-scale land acquisitions, it has typically been the investor who has captured attention: the western agribusiness or the Middle Eastern sovereign wealth fund, for example. What the Cambodian case illustrates is the role of the state in facilitating the transfer of land into the hands of a small class of owners. The idea that national governments necessarily represent the national interest when it comes to property ownership is facile. In many instances, they have openly ignored the demands of existing land-users for secure tenure and marketed land instead to international investors. For instance, the agricultural minister in Zambia once exclaimed that: 'We have well over thirty million hectares of land that is begging to be utilised . . . So far there hasn't been any of that resentment [to the sale of farmland]. If anything we are being told "You are too slow. When are these investors coming?"'[8]

The Zambian government certainly assisted in the expansion of Illovo's sugar operation in the country. As noted earlier, it granted the company tax breaks, access to cheap credit and guarantees of favourable sugar policy through an Investor Promotion and Protection Act. State-backed international donors have also played a role, with the EU and the African Development Bank providing a mixture of grant and loan finance to set up irrigated outgrower schemes that would allow additional village land to be converted to sugar cane.

Another case involving Illovo comes from Mali. In 1999, the US Agency for International Development (USAID) contracted the American company Schaffer and Associates to undertake a feasibility study for a sugar refinery in Mali's Office du Niger district. In total, US$2 million of

US-taxpayer money was provided to Schaffer by USAID and the US Trade and Development Agency. Schaffer subsequently formed the Société Sucrière de Markala (Sosumar), with Illovo as the majority owner.

In 2007, Schaffer, Illovo and the government of Mali signed a contract allocating Sosumar a fifty-year renewable lease on 17,000 hectares of land for sugar-cane plantations. Plans for the project began to divide communities, with many elders and other local elites in support and many villagers against it. While the concern among men was that they would lose their farmland, among women there was greater worry about the loss of communal shea trees, which were used to make butter, soap and medicine and provided an important source of income. Resistance to the project began to build, with a representative of the country's National Coordination of Peasants' Organizations, Ibrahima Coulibaly, even claiming that the lease itself was illegal under Malian law.[9]

Ironically, the major roadblock to the Sosumar's plans proved to be the inefficiency and collapse of the same government that approved them in the first place. In one of the cables later disclosed by Wikileaks, it was revealed that the American and South African Embassies in Mali had 'frequently raised concerns with senior Malian government officials' over the delays to the Sosumar project.[10] Ultimately, despite their best efforts to push the project through, in 2012 Illovo pulled out of the country. As well as the acute military conflict then raging, the company also cited the government's failure to provide infrastructure and concessional funding as reasons for its exit.

It is worth noting that even when investments fail, like the Sosumar project in Mali, damage can still be done to local communities. In 2006, a much-hyped 30,000-hectare sugar-cane project in Mozambique called ProCana began, but just five years later had collapsed. Nevertheless, tens of thousands of people due to be moved out of the newly created National Limpopo Park were left in limbo because some of the resettlement land meant for them was assigned to ProCana instead. Moreover, the plantation work that did begin had infringed on ring-fenced village land used for cattle grazing and charcoal production, disrupting the livelihoods of nearby residents. Worryingly for them, rather than reassess its approach to rural development after the failure of ProCana, in 2012 the Mozambican government simply granted the land concession to another investor, the South African sugar-cane group TSB.

In official statements, government ministers usually cite jobs and taxes as reasons to support large-scale commercial agriculture, although for reasons already stated these are often overestimated. What these ministers do not refer to are the political rationales for approving investment. One of these relates to the need to secure support from particular regions of the polity. During the reforms led by Deng Xiaoping in the 1980s, for instance, the Chinese government moved sugar production out of Guangdong and Fujian provinces and into Guangxi because the latter had inappropriate terrain for rice cultivation and a weak manufacturing base, making sugar one of the few remaining industries through which to deliver growth. In this way, the central government was able to win support from Communist Party officials in Guangxi who would benefit from the location of sugar production in their region and therefore be less likely to contest its broader project of 'opening up' coastal China.

Another attraction for state elites is the use of commercial agriculture as a political beachhead in remote 'outer territory'. The sugar estates and outgrower schemes established under General Suharto and funded by World

Bank loans in the 1970s can be seen in this light, when the Indonesian government's transmigration programme was moving millions of people from Java onto the more sparsely populated islands of Sumatra, Kalimantan and Sulawesi. This has been highly controversial, criticized by indigenous people living in these areas as a nationalist project designed to 'Javanize' the population and extend the power of the central Jakarta government. The permit acquired in 2010 by agribusiness Wilmar International to develop 200,000 hectares of land in the country's distant Papua province recalled many of these same tensions. While migrant farmers living in the area were generally open to investment, campaigners representing indigenous Papuans warned of 'the wholesale destruction and extermination of traditional communities' if the development were to go ahead.[11]

Finally, the fusion of financial interests between politicians and capitalists has added another dimension to government policy making. In 2014, the Zimbabwean government was accused by Human Rights Watch of purposely flooding out 3,000 families in the Tokwe-Mukorsi dam basin and withholding food aid from them unless they agreed to move to a sugar-cane estate and work the land there. The estate in question was owned by senior members of the ruling ZANU-PF party and the businessman and party supporter, Billy Rautenbach, who, incidentally, was also the initial investor in the ProCana project in Mozambique.

Taken together, what these cases show is that like the continued existence of bonded labour and child labour, the violent displacement of rural-dwelling people is no relic of history. Rather, the secular expansion of sugar-cane planting has required that ever more land be commodified to make space for the long-term investment in monocrop agriculture. Inevitably, this has led to the conversion of other property relations and land uses that still exist over much of the earth, including communal grazing land, collective forest land and usufruct subsistence land.

Nor is it just land on the farm that has been transformed. Where irrigation has been needed, pipelines, canals and occasionally dams have been established – usually paid for out of the public purse. Additional infrastructures to provide utilities (electricity lines, telephone masts), distribution services (roads, train lines, warehouses) and social services (employee housing, medical centres, country clubs) have also augmented the built environment. It is this connecting complex of fixed capital that lobbyists have often alluded to in their appeals for state support. As the geographer Gail Hollander found, industry boosters seeking government backing for land drainage and tariff protection in 1920s Florida did so in part by depicting the sugar town Clewiston as a 'Chicago in the Everglades' that would become 'the metropolis at the centre of a great and growing countryside'.[12] Fast-forward to the 2010s and a similar discourse can still be seen: green-field sugar-cane projects in Africa have been cast as a way to provide 'infrastructure and services development' for the 'degraded' rural hinterland.[13]

This is not to say that these developments are unequivocally bad. Better access to electricity, transport links, basic amenities and employment opportunities have generally been welcomed by those able to use them. But they have depended in one way or another on dislocating existing social and economic practices, and in gaining approval they have favoured some community representatives – like those of male chieftains and district officials – over others.

*The depletion and degradation of nature*
The previous section looked at the social dynamics of dis-possession and dislocation that have characterized the movement of the sugar frontier. We now look more closely at the environmental dynamics of this process, although it is important to bear in mind that the two cannot truly be separated. Any transformation of nature is at the same time a transformation in the conditions of production on which humans depend to produce goods and stay healthy, so for this reason many scholars prefer to think in terms of socio-ecological change. Specifically in the green Marxist tradition, it is the socio-ecological contradictions of capital-ism that are seen as the engine of historical change. So in the same way that the clearance of people from the country-side creates a transient mass seeking employment in urban areas, the simultaneous pollution of industrial towns from factories sucking in this rural raw material creates a bour-geois movement back the other way. Rare is the capitalist who lives on site.

The fusion of social and ecological inequalities can be readily discerned in the case of water. Sugar cane is fre-quently referred to as a thirsty crop; according to academics at Twente Water Centre, it is the sixth-biggest agricultural user of fresh water globally, with agriculture itself account-ing for 85 per cent of total surface and groundwater usage.[14] One consequence of sugar-cane production, then, has been to place additional demand on water availability, a deple-tion which has occasionally reached critical levels.

In 2013, Maharashtra was hit by a severe water shortage that withered crops, emaciated cattle and dried out taps. While the state government blamed the lack of rain, critics noted that the previous year had seen above-average rain-fall and with it the replenishment of reservoirs. In other words, absolute water scarcity was not apparent. According to the South Asia Network on Dams, Rivers and People, the cause of the problem was not bad weather but political mismanagement, in particular the historic decision to allow additional sugar-cane planting, which, by this point, was using 70 per cent of the state's irrigated water supply.[15] It was, in effect, a 'man-made drought'.

As with the commodification of land, the diversion of water from communal hydrological cycles into irrigation systems that privatize water usage has had widespread effects. In the Valle del Cauca region in Colombia, a research team led by Theresa Selfa found that the local sugar-cane industry had depleted the availability of water from underground wells, forcing some people to begin buying water for household use. In Pakistan, meanwhile, sugar-cane irrigation contributed to the reduced flow of river water to the Indus delta, which in turn led to a decline in fish and shrimp populations in its mangrove forests. The upshot for human life was the migration of millions of fishermen to the slums of Karachi in search of alternative work.

Depletion can also happen to the land itself. Soil erosion, combined with the continual removal of organic matter from the farm, has often outpaced the rate at which new soil is formed, leading to gradual loss in fertility and ultimately lower yields for the farmer. It was this logic of extraction that led Jason Clay of the World Wide Fund for Nature (WWF) to conclude that in most of the world, 'sugarcane production is little more than a "mining" operation that strips the resource base'.[16]

The second environmental consequence of sugar crop production is degradation, wherein natural resources are ruined and their use to other living beings impaired. In this respect, it is arguable that for water-based ecosystems, worse than the practice of taking water out has been allowing polluting substances back in. For instance, one of the reasons for the near collapse of the Great Barrier Reef in Australia has been the run-off of water and soil from adjacent sugar-cane farms, which is high in agro-chemicals. Among other things, this has led to algal blooms that have both reduced the amount of available oxygen to other living creatures (a process known as eutrophication) and provided food for the larvae of a coral-preying starfish, the malevolently named crown-of-thorns.

Water degradation has also stemmed from sugar mills and processors dumping untreated wastewater, known as effluent, into rivers. Research on the adverse effects of effluent on the Nzoia River in Kenya has been around since the 1970s, but, even as late as 2007, academic studies were reporting that water temperature, pH value and quality were still being affected by the ongoing activities of the Mumias Sugar Company mill, rendering the water unfit for human consumption and barely suitable for fish or plants either.[17]

Other natural resources that have been degraded by sugar production include soil and air. Soil health has suffered from compaction, flooding and salinity, spurring the need for the industry to constantly bring new and unspoiled land under cultivation. Air quality has been degraded by the burning of fossil fuels in the central mill/processor and the burning of sugar cane in the fields, although in this instance the cost has been largely borne by society. In Hawaii, for example, resident groups have formed to protest against what they call 'Maui snow' – the thick cloud of black ash that forms after cane burning – and the effects this has had on public health, from debilitating headaches to childhood asthma.

## Industrial agriculture and green growth

The reason why sugar production results in environmental damage is contested. For some, bad practices, like excessive fertilizer application, can simply be put down to a lack of information such as might be obtained from soil samples and weather forecasts, which could guide farmers as to how much fertilizer to apply and the best time to do it. Others put more weight on the continued use of 'primitive' technology which prevents more efficient use of natural resources and the ability to repair them in instances where they are damaged, such as the capture and cleaning of fertilizer-rich run-off before it reaches rivers and lakes. A third explanation is weak governance and the gaps in regulation that allow acts of environmental damage to go unpunished, like failing to monitor watercourses adjacent to sugar farms and to apply fines when people pollute them.

While each of these has merit, none of them properly accounts for the need to alter the environment in the first place. In keeping with the book's analysis thus far, this section argues that it is by virtue of their being *capitalist* organizations that imperatives are placed upon sugar producers to appropriate the 'free gifts of nature' and avoid paying the full social cost of using them. For example, the very reason why fertilizer is applied in the first place is to overcome limits to production set by soil fertility, which is also expensive and uncertain to maintain through traditional techniques like leaving land fallow or applying on-farm compost and animal manure. This is the hallmark of industrial agriculture: a system which constantly requires growth but cannot find the sources of growth within itself. In the same way that workers are exhausted and then replaced via the labour market, so too is the natural power of the land in the markets for fertilizer, farmland and water.

As the environmental historian Jason Moore has noted, this process is nothing new. Moving into native lands of the New World with their experimental form of plantation agriculture, colonial sugar planters were at first able to rely on ready supplies of local timber to power the boilers and construct the buildings, ships and barrels necessary to support long-distance trade.[18] However, as more and more forest was chopped down, timber soon became scarce and so had to be supplemented from other sources. Barbadian planters in the late seventeenth century began importing timber from British North America and even coal from across the Atlantic in Britain, before the prices of these began to eat into profitability and forced them to invest in new cane-crushing technology that would leave dry 'bagasse' stalks that they could burn instead.

But this was not the end of the problem. Replacing forests and indigenous flora with sugar cane exposed the soil to erosion, whilst killing off the fauna through habitat destruction and hunting had removed important sources of guano and dung. Again, as the land became less productive, planters looked outside for ways to renew it. One strategy was to introduce more livestock to the island for the express purpose of using their manure for fertilizer, but this only led to the clearing of more land for pasture and an accelerating cycle of fertility loss. Another strategy was to have the workforce carry washed-away soil back to the cane fields, although this too had a rebound effect as it meant that more costly slave labour had to be imported. In some cases, these strategies were fused. In 1689, the Barbadian sugar planter Edward Littleton recorded in his pamphlet 'The Groans of the Plantations' that 'some [of the planters] save the Urine of their People to increase and enrich their dung'.[19] In other words, in the endless effort to maintain yield, even the slaves' piss was made the property of their owner.

In essence, what was happening was that the pioneers of capitalist agriculture were attempting to simplify processes of nutrient cycling and reduce nature itself to a set of discrete inputs. However, each effort to boost land productivity caught on another contradiction that again undermined the conditions of production. The consequences of this 'sawtooth motion' were seismic. It gave the sugar-cane frontier its restless quality, as capitalists were not just lured to colonize new land by the prospect of *extra* profit but were actively pushed there by the need to *restore* it. As sugar-cane monoculture cycled through the tropical islands and coastal wetlands of the Americas (and now into its interior grasslands), it rendered whole ecosystems defunct. Such was the level of destruction that in his study of world agriculture, Jason Clay of the WWF argued that 'It is quite likely that the production of sugarcane has caused a greater loss of biodiversity on the planet than any other single agricultural crop'.[20]

It also set in train vast chains of ecological exchange. Along with the transatlantic slave trade, the intensive zones of capitalist sugar production also sucked in water, food, energy and raw materials from miles around. These natural resources were in turn 'embedded' in the sugar commodity and sent to the labouring classes in European towns. It was for this reason that Jason Moore concluded that colonial Barbados is best understood as an 'agricultural field of England', a peripheral region of the metropole whose overriding ecological function was to transfer nutrients to the core manufacturing regions which could no longer power themselves.[21]

In the contemporary period, two of the most important external inputs to sugar crop production have been agrochemicals and high-yielding seeds. Of the agro-chemicals, fertilizer represents the biggest market. As shown in

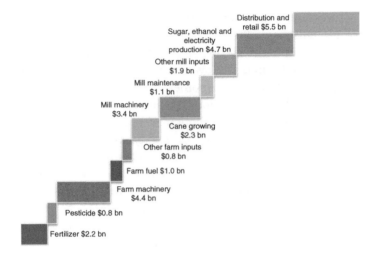

Figure 5.2 Brazilian sugar-cane value chain, 2008 (US$ billion)

*Note*: Figure shows the amount spent, inclusive of taxes, on different stages of production within the Brazilian sugar-cane industry.

*Source*: Author's adaptation of data in Marco Fava Neves, Vinicius Gustavo Trombin and Matheus Alberto Consoli (2010), 'Measurement of Sugar Cane Chain in Brazil', *International Food and Agribusiness Management Review* 13(3): 37–54.

Figure 5.2, the sugar-cane industry in Brazil alone spent US$2.2 billion on boosting the quantities of nitrogen, phosphate and potassium in its soils. In 2011, sugar cane was the biggest user of fertilizer in the entire country, reworking sugar's historic chains of ecological exchange. Fertilizers made from natural gas, phosphate rock and potash have all been imported into Brazil, bringing regions like Sichuan Province (China), Saskatchewan (Canada) and the Urals (Russia) into its production complex.

Like the colonial planters before them, the new masters of sugar-cane production – the internationalized milling groups based in São Paulo state – are also facing rising costs for replacing fertility. The International Sugar Organization has reported that the cost of fertilizer needed for a newly planted cane field in São Paulo jumped from US$434 per tonne in 2007 to US$674 in 2011.[22] One response by the mills has been to return to the traditional practice of pouring the potassium-rich by-product vinasse back on the fields, although they have had to contend with its side effects on soil health and poor seed germination (to say nothing of its polluting effects suffered by other land and water users). The Brazilian government, meanwhile, has taken a more direct route, encouraging the country's biggest mining company Vale to prospect for additional resources in Brazilian territory so as to secure cheap supplies of potash for domestic agribusiness.

Another external input to the sugar industry is seed, accounted for in Figure 5.2 in the category 'Other farm inputs'. In the wild, both sugar cane and sugar beet are reproduced through wind pollination. Under commercial cultivation, the process is more carefully controlled: new plants are grown from stem cuttings (for cane) and seeds (for beet) that have been specially bred for various traits, typically by separate off-farm organizations. And in the same way that commercial agriculture has sought to capitalize upon soil fertility and fresh water as productive resources, so too has it approached genetic diversity.

Historically, one of the most significant breeding stations was the Dutch Proefstation Oost Java in modern-day Indonesia. In the 1920s, it crossed the commercial species of sugar cane, *Saccharum officinarum*, with wild cane growing in Java to produce a variety that was less susceptible to disease. This variety, called POJ 2878, was soon sown across the majority of the island and also acquired by planters across the Americas to revive their ailing industries – although so successful was it in boosting yields that it had the perverse effect of encouraging overproduction and plunging the world sugar market back into a period of unbearably low prices. Socio-ecological contradiction strikes again.

One important shift in the provision of seed over the intervening years has been its steady commodification. Instead of being developed by state agencies and provided to all producers as a public good, new varieties of cane and beet have been developed by multinational biotechnology companies and treated as proprietary products. For example, two of the biggest cane-breeding stations in the world are CanaVialis and the Centro de Tecnologia Canavieira (CTC), both based in Brazil. The former was bought out by the American company Monsanto in 2008, while the latter signed cooperation agreements with the German companies BASF and Bayer in 2009–10 before then turning itself into a corporation with Copersucar and Raízen as its major shareholders.

The supposed benefit of privatizing research is that it accelerates technological development. As the director of plant science at the CTC has argued: 'Sugarcane research is normally funded by the government in other countries but this creates a system of subsistence research . . . just the minimum gets done and it's hard to make big breakthroughs.'[23] This might strike some as spurious. For instance, the research that allowed the CTC to sequence the sugar-cane genome during the early 2000s and patent its sugar-producing genes was largely funded by the state of São Paulo. This brings to mind the concern of food studies scholar Geoff Tansey, who has noted the shift in agricultural R&D towards the pharmaceutical model.[24] Here, according to Tansey, instead of being directed to farm-based practical innovations, public subsidies are directed towards laboratory-based innovation. Moreover, any commercial application is then claimed as private property, enforced at the global level through the Trade-Related Aspects of Intellectual Property Rights agreement of the WTO and backed up by its dispute settlement mechanism.

Another concern with the commodification of seeds – now heightened by the patenting of genetic material itself – is that it is transferring wealth away from farming and towards input provision. This has happened, firstly, through the commercialization of seed distribution, and secondly, by linking the sale of seeds to sales of agro-chemicals. For example, to make sure that its powerful weedkiller Roundup® does not also damage crops, Monsanto has bred herbicide-resistant Roundup Ready® seeds that are then sold together as a package. The efficacy of this technological package has been questioned. The Center for Food Safety has argued that in the United States, where it has been widely adopted for sugar beets, the seed–chemical combination has only led to the evolution of herbicide-resistant weeds and, once again, another negative feedback effect.[25]

For sugar farmers, who dare not stop spraying Roundup for fear that crops will be completely lost to weeds, this means buying more herbicide. At the time of writing, the US Environmental Protection Agency was deciding whether to increase the limit for agro-chemical application in order to make this legally permissible. For farmers of other crops, who opposed the introduction of genetically modified sugar beet on the basis that it might cross-pollinate with their own organic produce and destroy their market value, the result has been protracted legal battles. One such farmer was Frank Morton, who sought a court injunction against the US Department of Agriculture for failing to conduct an environmental impact assessment of Roundup Ready sugar beet. This provided a temporary reprieve, but the assessment was conducted and the seeds began to be released. Trying instead for a complete prohibition, after three years of wrangling the plaintiffs were ultimately denied because they could not prove they would suffer 'irreparable harm' from the release of the GM seeds. In a related court case that must have really stuck in the craw of organic farmers, Monsanto refused to rule out *suing them* for 'using' the company's patented genetic material as a result of inadvertent cross-pollination.

There are two points to take from this discussion of the capitalist thrust towards industrial agriculture. The first is the tendency for mechanical, chemical and genetic innovations to be articulated together and transform the way that land *and* labour are used. For example, in 1960s Britain, tractors (mechanical technology) were used to sow monogerm seeds (genetic technology) which were then sprayed with herbicides (chemical technology). This not only provided a temporary boost to yields but also replaced the work previously done by hand to 'thin out' the weaker shoots of the sugar beet and remove nearby weeds. More recently in 2010s Brazil, the Swiss biotechnology company Syngenta began marketing its PLENE™ package. Based on cane stems which were smaller and pre-treated with chemicals – which therefore could be planted mechanically and avoid a subsequent pesticide spraying – the package was sold to the industry as a way to boost yields through more regular replanting since it would now be cheaper and quicker to do.[26]

The second point is that, while these innovations have created increased uniformity in the production process, secular yield growth remains elusive. As shown in Figure 5.3, the sawtooth motion of land productivity remains apparent. This can be attributed in part to the negative feedback effects described previously and in part to the fluctuations in conditions that industrial capital has yet to bring com-

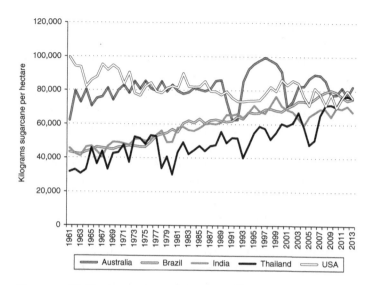

Figure 5.3 Yield sugar cane per hectare, 1961–2013

*Source*: FAOSTAT

pletely under its control, such as temperature, rainfall and uneven land. Moreover, at the national level, the convergence towards 80,000 kilograms of sugar cane produced per hectare suggests that a plateau may have been reached. The promise held out by genetic engineering – practised in the North American sugar-beet industry since 2007 and trialled in various sugar cane-growing countries – is to transcend this limit. Like new fertile land, genetic material is a frontier in which the free gifts of nature can be appropriated. But by the same token, as we noted earlier, it does not boost productivity in perpetuity. The best it can provide is a temporary fix to an enduring problem.

There is a final twist to the environmental history of sugar production. In many countries, the combination of rising fossil fuel prices and criticism of the depletion and degradation of nature has created possibilities for the production of 'green' commodities. One of the most important in relation to sugar crops has been biofuel. In Brazil, the world leader in sugar-cane biofuels, 21 per cent of the country's transport fuel came from ethanol in 2011, helped by extensive state support in the form of blend mandates, tax breaks, subsidized credit and R&D support. Justifying this support, the government has claimed that, since 1975, the use of biofuel has saved the country US$137 billion in oil payments and 550 million tonnes of carbon dioxide emissions.[27]

Sugar-cane ethanol is now also finding its way into other oil-based products such as plastic, and its production from the inedible leaves and stalks of the plant (known as cellulosic ethanol) appears to be on the brink of commercialization. Another source of revenue is electricity. By investing in boilers and generators to burn the leftover biomass, many mills and processors are now able to meet their own energy needs and even export electricity to the grid. Indeed, more than one hundred of these projects, mainly in Brazil and India, have been certified by the UN's Clean Development Mechanism and awarded carbon credits that the mills can sell to traders operating in the EU carbon market.

The claims about the amount of carbon emissions saved by using cane- or beet-based feedstock instead of fossil fuels are controversial, as we shall see below. Nevertheless, there has been a definite trend for mills and processors to capitalize on every bit of biomass and reinvent themselves as 'more-than-sugar' producers. For instance, British Sugar now refers to one of its sugar-processing factories as a 'bio-refinery . . . a model of advanced and sustainable manufacturing'.[28] In this bio-refinery, even the heat generated in the sugar production process is put to use, sent to greenhouses which grow 140 million tomatoes a year. Others have gone further still, with Brazilian sugar-cane company Cosan declaring its intent to move away from sugar and become 'focused on the infrastructure and energy sectors'.[29]

For its advocates, then, this vision of industrial agriculture offers a vital source of 'green growth', a way to create clean energy and provide technical jobs. For its detractors, this is hyperbole. It remains reliant on external inputs, has questionable carbon savings and shifts the share of the distribution of wealth in rural farming even further towards industrial capital.

*Social activism*

To reiterate an earlier point, the way that land and nature are woven into the production of sugar and ethanol is a socio-ecological issue. Thus reaction to its expansionary, industrial character can be found in a diverse array of actors, including human rights advocates, development campaigners, wildlife enthusiasts and community action groups. Unlike labourers, who have a vested economic interest in the survival of the industry, these social activists have greater autonomy from sugar-based capital and often adopt more antagonistic positions towards it.

One example of this was the public attack on biofuels in the mid-2000s, which in the EU was fronted by international environmental and development groups, including ActionAid, Friends of the Earth, Greenpeace and Oxfam. There were two prongs to this opposition. One concerned the adverse effects on levels of global hunger as biofuel demand diverted crops into non-food markets. The other concerned the effects on greenhouse gas emissions as this same diversion also encouraged land to be converted to agricultural production, either through direct or indirect land-use change, thus invalidating their 'environmentally friendly' claim. Direct land-use change refers to the land being used to grow the biofuel crops; indirect land-use change refers to the conversion of land somewhere else as a result of biofuel production, e.g. a farmer in another country expanding his arable land to fill the supply gap in a food market.

Since the political argument for biofuel mandates in the EU had been based on the need to provide clean energy, debates quickly came to rest on what the 'real' carbon footprint of biofuels was and whether this justified extensive state support. As shown in Table 5.2, while sugar-based biofuel generally received a clean bill of health, other crops did not. This was thanks to the biological efficiencies of cane and beet in producing fermentable sugars, the smaller amounts of oil and fertilizer used in their production, and the reduced risk that growing sugar crops would lead to ecologically destructive land conversion elsewhere. It should be mentioned, however, that all these findings were hotly contested. After the European Commission staff working document was released, suggesting that using biodiesel would be worse for the environment than sticking with petroleum, the biodiesel association shot back saying there were 'critical data errors and important methodological problems' with measuring the effects of indirect land-use change which rendered the Commission's GHG savings arbitrary.[30]

The upshot in the EU was a cap applied to the amount of biofuel that could come from food crops and a concomitant shift in support towards those made from inedible plant material (so-called second-generation or cellulosic biofuels). But, in a sop to the industry, the Commission also agreed that the new greenhouse gas emissions-savings figures, which included the estimated effects of indirect land-use change, would not apply to biofuel suppliers and

Table 5.2 Estimates of the greenhouse gas (GHG) emissions savings of different biofuels

| Biofuel | GHG Savings | Source |
|---|---|---|
| Sugar-cane ethanol | 61 per cent | US Environmental Protection Agency 2010 Renewable Fuel Standard[31] |
| | 54 per cent | European Commission 2012 Staff Working Document[32] |
| | 54 per cent | IFPRI 2010[33] |
| Sugar-beet ethanol | 56 per cent | European Commission 2012 Staff Working Document |
| | 36 per cent | IFPRI 2010 |
| Corn ethanol | 47 per cent | European Commission 2012 Staff Working Document |
| | 21 per cent | US Environmental Protection Agency 2010 Renewable Fuel Standard |
| | 4 per cent | IFPRI 2010 |
| Rapeseed biodiesel | −5 per cent | European Commission 2012 Staff Working Document |
| Soybean biodiesel | −13 per cent | European Commission 2012 Staff Working Document |

Note: GHG savings include estimates for indirect land-use change.

that minimum savings would still be calculated on the old, less contentious model.

The effect of these decisions was to smooth over the differences between different crops in terms of their emissions savings and this penalized sugar-based biofuels as much as it did those based on rapeseed. However, for the more ardent critics – including radical environmental organizations – even this compromise was insufficient. For their part, the whole biofuel project merely prolonged reliance on fossil-fuel powered vehicles and detracted from necessary structural change such as electrifying the transport fleet and investing in better town planning and public transport to reduce the demand for fuel in the first place.

To the extent that this activism sought to roll back the introduction of a single policy (i.e. biofuel consumption mandates), it can be characterized as defensive. It was also transnational in organization, with lobbying activity by groups in Europe drawing on links with their grassroots affiliates to highlight the repercussions of biofuel production on people in the Global South. Another defensive, transnational campaign can be seen in Cambodia, where community groups and domestic charities formed the Clean Sugar Campaign to protest against the illegal land concessions used to grow sugar and demand proper restitution for those dispossessed. However, this campaign can be differentiated in two important respects.

First, it has focused on reversing a series of practices, rather than one specific policy, and so has adopted a wider array of targets and tactics. Second, because the Cambodian government has been complicit in the very problem of land dispossession, the campaign has embraced 'boomerang' activism, appealing to actors outside their political constituency to alter practices within it. This has produced a multifaceted campaign which has included: shaming financiers like Deutsche Bank into divesting from the sugar plantations; filing complaints with the National Human Rights Commission of Thailand to investigate the practices of its investing firms; suing Tate & Lyle in the United Kingdom for knowingly importing illegally produced sugar; using the grievance mechanism of the standard-setting organization Bonsucro to identify non-compliances by its members Mitr Phol and Tate & Lyle; and pressurizing the EU to suspend its trade preferences to Cambodian sugar until a proper human rights investigation has been conducted.

These interventions have secured important victories: small offers of recompense and alternative land have been made by the government, and at the time of writing the European Commission is investigating reparations claims made by villagers evicted with inadequate compensation. However, coming three years into the campaign and nine years since the first evictions began, it is clear that much of the damage has already been done. In the meantime, the sugar industry remains largely unaffected and the injustices committed in its name still unaccounted for.

In contrast to these two campaigns stands the long-running struggle to restore the Everglades ecosystem in Florida. This has been offensive in that it has aimed to restructure the region's sugar industry and actively renew the wetlands. It has also been organized on a sub-national basis – coalescing in civic associations like the Friends of the Everglades and local chapters of conservation groups like the Audubon Society and the Sierra Club – although as Gail Hollander has noted, it has periodically 'jumped scale' to become a national issue, especially during presidential elections when politicians have needed to court the Florida vote.[34]

In the last twenty years, there have been two major legislative acts made in response to this activism. The first was the Everglades Forever Act of 1994, which was a state-level piece of legislation designed to ratchet up the regulatory duties undertaken by Florida's environment and water agencies. Like the sugar-cane industry in Australia, cane growers in Florida stood accused of allowing polluted water to run off into the watercourses of a sensitive ecosystem, but efforts to pass on some of the clean-up costs to the industry in the form of taxes or environmental liability payments were forcefully resisted. More headway was made in limiting future degradation. According to legal scholar Alfred Light, the obligation for cane growers to implement Best Management Practices and farm-level monitoring techniques, in combination with check-ups by district officials, has since been successful in reducing the discharge of phosphorous fertilizer into the Everglades.[35]

The second legislative act was the Comprehensive Everglades Restoration Plan (CERP) of 2000, designed to capture clean fresh water and redirect it to the parched wetlands, as well as the state's expanding cities. It was hugely ambitious: at its launch, US$13.5 billion was pledged for projects over the next thirty years, with funding split between the federal and Florida state governments. One of these projects came to include a buy-out of US Sugar Corporation land located on the former site of the fabled 'River of Grass', the shallow river that had once flowed from Lake Okeechobee to what was now designated as the Everglades National Park. In 2008, US$1.75 billion was earmarked for the buy-out, to be borrowed by the South Florida Water Management District.

However, falling property taxes and budget cuts in the wake of the sub-prime mortgage crash scaled down the acquisition. In 2010, US$197 million was spent on just 26,800 acres of US Sugar's 179,800 acre property. Moreover, US Sugar has since requested approval to develop some of its remaining land for housing and commercial use, an urbanization on the banks of Lake Okeechobee hardly in keeping with the wider environmental effort. In addition, activists have warned that, even if the development does not go ahead, planning approval would push up the cost to the Florida taxpayer of acquiring the remaining land for the 'River of Grass' project, the same taxpayer that has already paid the vast majority of the total US$2 billion cost of the Everglades clean-up to date.[36]

## Governing land

As we have seen in the preceding three examples, social activists have invoked state power to mediate between capital and nature. They have done so to change both how land is used (e.g. for food production, for subsistence, for conservation) and how it should be governed (e.g. suspending biofuel mandates, restituting 'grabbed' land, reducing agro-chemical application and relocating sugar cane). In each case, at least some businesses in the sugar industry staunchly opposed the proposed measures. Yet not all interventions in the 'production of nature' have been antagonistic to industry interests.

An example here would be the land-use policies introduced in Brazil during the 2000s, which included a federal zoning programme to direct sugar-cane planting into designated areas and state-level programmes to phase out cane burning and protect riparian areas. Whilst placing some restrictions on expansion, these programmes also helped to market Brazilian biofuel as a global commodity, feeding into those earlier assessments of its carbon footprint and its general image as a clean, green fuel. This explains the high level of industry support for the programmes, alongside the fact that sugar producers had successfully prevented the government from giving the zoning rules retrospective bite (meaning the land-use restrictions were not applied to land already planted or licensed to plant sugar cane).

State mediation of the way land is incorporated into capital accumulation has also taken place at the international level. Recalling Hollander's observation about land politics 'jumping scale' at crucial moments, in the context of heated activism around the global land grab, various international initiatives to govern agricultural land investment shot to prominence. Two of the most important were led by the World Bank and the UN's Committee on World Food Security (CFS).

In 2010, the World Bank announced its 'Principles for Responsible Agricultural Investment', aimed chiefly at private investors in international land markets. These principles included respecting land and resource rights, ensuring that investments do not jeopardize food security, consulting affected people and promoting better assessments of project sustainability. In 2012, this was followed by the CFS's 'Voluntary Guidelines on Responsible Governance of Tenure of Land, Fisheries and Forests', which were aimed instead at the governments of countries with large agrarian populations.

One salient point made in both documents was that land zoning can do more harm than good if some classifications of land as 'ecologically significant' or 'indigenous territory' produce converse categories of 'ecologically insignificant' and 'unoccupied territory' then touted for investment. As noted in the World Bank's Principles: 'It is important to recognize that there are few areas truly "unoccupied" or "unclaimed", and that frequently land classified as such is in fact subject to long-standing rights of use, access and management based on custom.'[37]

But, in other respects, the initiatives differed. While many of the same organizations, such as the UN's Food and Agricultural Organization, contributed to both processes, the CFS also received input from international peasant movements and rural human rights groups. As a result of this participation, as well as the differing philosophies of their respective bureaucracies, the CFS's Guidelines advanced two additional demands. First, they focused on securing rights for land-users first, rather than abiding by those patchwork laws and deeds that currently exist. Second, not content to simply protect rural dwellers from the worst effects of industrial agriculture, they actively endorsed alternatives to this through agrarian reforms.[38]

In terms of *how* they would govern, the CFS's Guidelines and the World Bank's Principles again shared fundamental similarities. They both relied on voluntary implementation. To encourage governments to translate their frameworks into domestic policy, the signatories of these documents proposed linking them to lending decisions by international organizations, promised to undertake capacity building in key host countries to introduce and enforce supporting legislation, and pledged to establish consensus among investors about socially acceptable practice. But, ultimately, in so far as neither initiative has been able to *impose* itself on the way land is legally administered by state authorities, question marks remain hanging over the effectiveness of each.

It is in this respect that the governance mechanism contained in the EU's Renewable Energy Directive is so interesting. Passed in 2009, the directive required that all biofuels sold in the EU meet certain environmental criteria, such as not being produced from crops grown on wetland, peat land, primary forest or biodiverse grassland. Moreover, compliance with these criteria would be monitored through audits undertaken by private-sector certification bodies approved by the EU. Thus, rather than relying on other states to ensure that 'ecologically significant' land was not being razed to make way for biofuel plantations, this system seemed to offer a more robust way of monitoring production practices and enforcing compliance with them, i.e. through threat of disqualification from the EU biofuel market.

There were certainly some limitations to this directive. Covering only environmental criteria in biofuel investments, it was much narrower in scope than the principles and guidelines mentioned above. This was a conscious decision by the European Commission. Earlier calls for it to include social criteria in its assessment of 'legitimate biofuels' had been ignored because of the belief that any attempt to include land rights or labour standards would trigger a dispute at the WTO by biofuel exporters claiming they were being unfairly discriminated against. Applying *environmental* criteria, meanwhile, was considered fair game since the EU had only mandated biofuel consumption in the first place to lower greenhouse gas emissions.

There have also been criticisms of the certification systems designed to monitor land-use change. Like the problems that befell the 'National Commitment to Enhance Working Conditions in Sugarcane' in Brazil, reports have surfaced of poor-quality audits, with the environmental law group ClientEarth even taking the European Commission to court for failing to justify the approval of less scrupulous certification systems. Nevertheless, what the EU Renewable Energy Directive did demonstrate was that it was possible for state regulation to purposely reach into other jurisdictions, meaning that the politically challenging task of negotiating binding international treaties was not the only way in which land law could be globalized.

Another form of land governance that has stretched across borders has been corporate self-regulation and social responsibility. This has sought to bypass the state altogether, ostensibly putting the tasks of enforcing existing law and evolving best practice into the hands of multinational companies themselves, which are then expected to filter this down through their respective supply chains. There are two main reasons why companies have voluntarily undertaken these tasks and accepted their designation as moral actors.

The first has been to restore the conditions of production

on which they depend for continued accumulation. In this respect, capitalist organizations have functioned as if they were the state, addressing their own contradictions to protect otherwise threatened profits. The second reason has been to legitimize the way in which they accumulate wealth, lest social criticism build to the extent that states are compelled to regulate their activities for them or consumers refuse to buy their products. Both these rationales can be seen in the recent initiatives of Coca-Cola.

In 2004 and 2014, Coca-Cola bottling plants in Kerala and Uttar Pradesh were shut down by Indian state governments, following public complaints that the company had breached their licences and depleted local water tables. To make sure it has continued access to fresh water for use in its plants and on the sugar-cane fields, the company has thus engaged in a number of public–private partnerships. One of these is in Guangxi province in China. Launched in 2010 with the UN Development Programme and the national and state governments, this was a US$3.5 million investment – with Coca-Cola funding the US$0.5 million – in wastewater treatment and water-saving 'drip irrigation' technology.[39] Likewise, in 2013 and following a targeted campaign by Oxfam, the company declared 'zero tolerance' for land grabbing, pledging that it would only buy sugar grown from consensually acquired land and that all its sugar suppliers would be independently certified by 2020.

As the world's biggest buyer of sugar, Coca-Cola has significant financial leverage over its suppliers, although the messy reality of trying to save resources and safeguard rights suggests that we should not put too much faith in the ability of a single organization to achieve such goals. Moreover, as progressive as these goals might seem, it is important to remember that they are ultimately predicated on the continued use of water and land for the production of marketized soft drinks. Whether this corporate pursuit is a valid use of socio-ecological resources should remain up for debate, even when (or especially when) accompanied by self-declared responsible behaviour.

## Conclusion

For industrial capital engaged in agriculture, a constant problem has been how to control the means of production. To the extent that landowners charge extortionate rents and nature limits or disrupts the production process, sugar mills and processors cannot be assured of sufficient profits. This chapter has outlined a number of ways in which resolution of this problem has been attempted. These were bringing in natural resources from outside the existing relations of private property through 'land grabbing' and genetic patenting, ending the separation between land-owner and producer through mill-owned farmland and outgrower schemes, and eliminating the traditional basis of agriculture through the use of external inputs.

Spurred by the rising world market prices for food and fuel and enabled by the glut of mobile finance capital, such investments accelerated markedly during the early 2000s. They did so mainly in the Global South, in locations chosen as much for the pliability of their political authorities as for their comparative advantage in climate or land quality. The human impacts wrought by this transformation of the countryside have been profound. Traditional livelihoods, community ties and public health have all been threatened, although, by the same token, the provision of some waged jobs and infrastructure has offered what many consider to be the essence of rural development, especially when combined with ring-fenced protection of ecologically sensitive areas. This is development based on a stark bifurcation of land: on the one hand, industrial farming monocultures devoid of biodiversity and, on the other hand, conservation zones devoid of humans.

A key political issue has been the extent to which the sugar industry has been held responsible for these changes. We saw how various kinds of social activists – from international charities to local resident associations – have sought to hold it to account for socio-ecological damage by appealing to the state to mediate between capital and nature. But we also saw how capitalists have had to face down the depletion and degradation of nature for their own sake since the constant quest for growth has created feedback effects undermining this very process. This contradiction has long plagued the business of sugar production and will continue to do so. How it will be resolved, however, remains an open question and one we ponder in the final chapter.

# CHAPTER SIX

# A Sweeter Deal for All?

The last four chapters have traced the passage of the sugar commodity through three key moments: its consumption, exchange and production. Along the way, critical political dynamics have been highlighted. The chapter on consumption argued that sugar has helped dissolve barriers to accumulation, allowing food manufacturers and retailers to break down established dietary structures and sell more products. This gave them a powerful incentive to promote the continued consumption of sugar through coordinated cultural manipulation, even in the face of mounting evidence from the medical establishment around its ill effects.

The chapter on exchange argued that the rules of international trade have been essential to determining the kind of markets in which food sugar and fuel ethanol are sold, and thereby how the proceeds of accumulation are distributed. Moves by state authorities towards the liberalization of trade and investment flows have made it easier for global capital to profit from their exchange whilst simultaneously limiting the policy space previously used to protect domestic producers.

Finally, the chapters on production argued that labour and land have been treated in similar ways under capitalist agriculture: exploited and exhausted in the unending quest to earn more money. But the precise way in which this has been carried out has differed, shaped by the boom-and-bust dynamics and prevailing political consensus in particular places – the latter forged largely by opposition from organized labour and social activists to the industry's most abusive practices.

Across each of these political dynamics, different alliances and antagonisms were identified *between* industry actors. For instance, while food manufacturers and sugar millers have worked together to defend sugar against the criticisms of health advocates, they have also clashed over trade regulation and the pricing structure this implied. Likewise, while sugar millers and farmers have presented a united front to governments in order to influence national state policy, they have also fallen out over price negotiations related to the annual crop payment. As a last example, while sugar producers and corn producers have both supported the construction of biofuel markets, they have frequently disagreed over the dietary guidelines and production quotas governing sweetener markets.

What this shows is that the commonplace reference to 'the sugar lobby' can be easily misused since, depending on the point in question, there might be as much that divides businesses as unites them. The political economist André Drainville offers a helpful conceptual device here, distinguishing between 'cliques of capital' temporarily brought together by support for a particular policy and 'fractions of capital' whose common interests are incorporated in a multi-layered and long-term strategy organized through trade associations, pressure groups and links with political parties and state departments.[1] This book has highlighted the crucial role played by the *industrial* fraction of capital – as opposed to, say, landed capital or commercial capital – in the way that sugar has been produced, priced and consumed. The shared interests of primary processors and final food manufacturers in the mass production of sweet industrial foods was the great unifying project of sugar politics in the twentieth century.

At the same time, the book has also showed how these power structures are in the process of change. The steady evolution of sugar-cane millers and sugar-beet processors into 'bio-refineries' intent on producing a range of renewable raw materials has brought them into partnership with both oil companies and biotechnology companies. One consequence of this shift has been to link the markets for food and energy more closely together. Higher prices for oil and other fossil fuels no longer just affect the cost of fertilizers and running farm machinery; they also encourage sugar-cane millers (particularly those in Brazil) to produce more ethanol and less sugar, putting a second inflationary pressure on the world price of sugar.

Another consequence has been to *de*-link traditional marketing channels between crops and food. For example, the joint venture Vivergo Fuels in the United Kingdom, between British Sugar, BP and DuPont, is intended to process wheat not into bread flour but into ethanol fuel and animal feed. Final food manufacturers have also advanced this de-linking process by searching for alternative sources of sweetness. A popular alternative since the late 2000s has been to use compounds extracted from the leaf of the stevia plant, which, unlike corn syrups and artificial sweeteners, allows both 'zero calorie' *and* 'all natural' claims to be made. Stevia leaves have long been dried, ground and added to drinks and medicines by the Guaraní peoples of South America (the same people being alienated from their land in part because of sugar-cane production). But consistent with our story of industrial agriculture, this artisanal processing has been reworked such that Cargill, in partnership with biotechnology firm Evolva, can now create the sweet-stevia compounds through microbial fermentation in the laboratory rather than rely on farmers, and the stevia plant, to do it out in the field. In short, the dynamics of substitutionism have weakened the common interest between industrial capitals engaged in agro-food production in the singular pursuit of sugar-sweetened diets.

As well as changes to the interests of sugar by industrial capital, there have also been changes in its composition. Among primary processors, there has been significant concentration, with millers and processors taking over existing facilities and expanding through new ones. In 2012, the top ten producers of sugar were Südzucker, Associated British Foods, Raízen, Tereos, Mitr Phol, Nordzucker, Thai Roong Ruang, Wilmar, Louis Dreyfus and Pfiefer & Langen.[2] As revealed in their annual reports, many of these have grown by investing outside their home countries, becoming truly multinational companies. Südzucker's operating profit in its sugar division was 511 million euros but only one-third of its sugar production was in Germany.[3] Likewise, Associated British Foods showed an operating profit of £510 million, with just one-quarter of its sugar production taking place in Britain.[4]

Much foreign investment has taken place in Brazil, with Tereos, among others, buying up processing capacity in the country to produce ethanol as well as sugar.[5] In 2006, just 3 per cent of the milling capacity in Brazil was foreign-owned; by 2012, this had jumped to 33 per cent.[6] As we saw in chapter 3, this 'foreignization' has helped to push smaller family-owned mills to the margins and to concentrate the industry into a handful of highly capitalized and increasingly internationalized firms.

Such cross-border investments have also precipitated vertical integration in the sugar supply chain, with traders and millers/processors joining forces through equity investment, joint ventures and long-term contracts. Some of the most significant deals have been between Cargill and Copersucar in 2014 and ED&F Man and Südzucker in 2012 (both focused on the marketing side) and between Wilmar and Sucrogen in 2010 and Louis Dreyfus and Santelisa Vale in 2009 (both focused on the production side). Notwithstanding the problems faced by some traders in penetrating the sugar industry – recall Bunge's difficulties in Brazil – this has raised the prospect that commercial capital will come to dominate sugar and ethanol in the same way it has other commodities, seizing control of the exchanges between farmers and final food manufacturers and charging fees along the way.

What all this goes to show is that the organization of the sugar industry is not static. Inter-capitalist conflict will continue to drive change of its own accord as different businesses build their profitability as fast as they can. However, this does not happen in a bubble. As shown throughout this book, health professionals, state planners, organized labour and social activists have all pushed and pulled on the accumulation process, shaping the bounds of permissible practice. This is consistent with the book's theoretical foundations: that the circulation of sugar is deeply structured by global capitalism, but that capitalism need not be a single fate.

In the remainder of this chapter, we consider how sugar provisioning could become more ecologically sound and socially just. Organized around four key demands – for healthy eating, fair exchange, empowered working and diverse land – it outlines some strategies that have sought to reform capitalist practices and others that subverted its very principles of private property and profiteering. None of these offer a universal solution to the problems of sugar; each must be tailored to its context and try to avoid replacing one set of oppressive relations with another. Moreover, none of them will be willingly accepted by those currently benefiting from the status quo. In this respect, the chapter title is a bit misleading: there is no 'sweeter deal' for *all*, only for some. What they do offer are instantiations of critical sugar politics, showing the willingness of people to challenge the predominant institutional structures of the economy *and* their capacity to remake them along alternative lines.

## Healthy eating

What are the vectors of transformation around sugar consumption? One is the call for state protection from excessive corporate marketing. This has coalesced around the notion of consumer rights and appears to offer a solid moral and legal platform on which to make further challenges. In 2014, for example, the Canadian health minister proposed to make the information about added sugars in on-product labels much clearer, while, in the state of California, one senator backed by public health groups sought to mirror anti-smoking legislation by proposing that sugar-sweetened drinks be made to carry warning labels for obesity, diabetes and tooth decay.

As well as revealing information about sugared products, consumer protection initiatives have also sought to restrict claims made about them. In 2011, the UK Advertising Standards Authority upheld complaints by members of the public who contested claims made by Coca-Cola that its vitamin-water drink could be called 'nutritious', given the amount of sugar it contained. The advert was banned and the following year the company reduced the amount of calories in the product by reformulating it with stevia. And, again in California, claims made against one company for calling sugar 'evaporated cane juice' on its list of ingredients and another for labelling chocolate spread as 'healthy' have also been upheld in court.

Advertising sugar-laden foods to children has come in for particular censorship, trading on the idea that as children they have not developed the kind of consumer rationality that will allow them to make informed decisions. In Australia, the Fat Free TV Guide allows parents to identify programmes that heavily advertise food high in salt, sugar and fat so they can be taken out of the family's viewing schedule; in the United Kingdom, campaigners have called for a complete ban on such adverts until after the 9 pm watershed.

At its most extreme, this kind of argument has led to court cases by individuals alleging that sugar and sweetener companies have knowingly sold them harmful products. In 2014, a federal court in the United States heard a case against Archer Daniels Midland for producing high fructose corn syrup, allegedly a substantial factor in a 14-year-old girl developing Type II diabetes. The case was dismissed but other legal challenges, particularly class actions by financially beleaguered health departments, will surely follow in its train.

In these attempts to restrict sugar consumption by emphasizing its adverse effects on health, reformers may find themselves aided by another set of powerful companies. To help them sell more drugs, the pharmaceutical industry has sought to widen the diagnosis of diseases like diabetes and to turn conditions like obesity into diseases. In 2013, the American Medical Association concurred and decided that obesity would now be categorized as a disease rather than a risk factor for other diseases, potentially increasing the amount of state research funding and insurance pay-outs allocated to it.

As part of this 'medicalization' of eating and in the spirit of nutritionism which we mentioned in chapter 2, novel foods are also being developed. Targeting those with diabetes, Nestlé has launched BOOST® Glucose Control and Resource® Diabetic – drinks and supplements to meet specific nutritional needs. It is even trying to find a way of modulating enzymes in the human body so that people who are old, diabetic or obese can burn more calories from the same amount of exercise. Bear in mind that this is the same company that has continued to lobby for cheaper access to sugar, noting in its 2012 evidence to the UK House of Lords that: 'A large manufacturing organisation such as Nestlé, Coke or other organisations, will consume vast quantities of sugar on a daily basis, so we need a really good, strong infrastructure of available [suppliers] bringing in two, three, four, five or six lorries' worth of sugar per day.'[7] Putting aside the irony of a company selling both sin and salvation, what this points towards is the rise of the *post-industrial* food, one which is designed and produced in conjunction with the consumer, tailored to their individual needs.

Part of this changing commodity relation involves the development of drug foods like weight management formulas (note the different meaning of drug food than previously discussed), another part the commercialization of feminized lifestyle trends like 'No Fructose' and 'Zero Sugar' diets through the media. Finally, this individuation of consumption both encourages and is enabled by daily practices of self-surveillance, in which bio-markers such as blood sugar levels, calorific intake and body mass indexes are constantly monitored. This is being further aided by life-logging internet technologies like 'smart' forks and cups, which can calculate how much sugar is in your meal and record the data for you, your online community, your doctor or your health insurer to act upon.[8]

If all this sounds quite worrying, it is meant to. While the notion of using consumer rights to reduce sugar intake has its benefits, to the extent that it opens the door to medicalization and retains a focus on the body as a site of accumulation, it only creates another set of problems. One is that it treats dietary issues privately in the clinic/hospital, rather than seeking to prevent them through public health programmes. These are focused instead on the universal provision of healthy foods and the restructuring of fat-inducing 'obesogenic environments', such as moving high-sugar foods away from supermarket checkouts or congregating them all in a designated aisle. Another is that the unending projects of self-improvement levy an acute psychological toll on individuals, particularly those who already fall into stigmatized categories of bodily failure.

A different approach to challenging patterns of sugar consumption can be discerned in things like home-cookery programmes, campaigns for healthy school meals and the Slow Food movement. None of these target sugar consumption per se but rather advance forms of food provisioning that are less dependent on market exchange and are therefore less exposed to the appeal of heavily sweetened convenience industrial foods. While there is no guarantee that foods made in the home or ordered by a public body will necessarily contain less sugar or be eaten in moderation, if people are reconnected with what they are ingesting and diets are divested of the profit motive, established social norms like viewing sweetened foods as treats rather than staples might well reassert themselves. To this end, and following the suggestion of anthropologist Claude Fischler, research on those societies that have historically *restrained* their sugar consumption, rather than intensified it, could provide insights into how this might be achieved.[9]

Like the previous agenda, though, this also has its

risks. It can fall into romanticism, promoting a return to pre-industrial foods and the gender biases on which this provisioning operated. It might also become the privilege of the affluent and, much like the bodily aesthetic, inflict what the sociologist Pierre Bourdieu called symbolic violence upon those who do not conform to its moral strictures.[10] The celebrity chef Jamie Oliver found himself attacked for wielding such a weapon when he denigrated low-income families in the United Kingdom for eating junk food in front of a 'massive TV', rather than cooking cheap traditional dishes as they do in Italy or Spain.[11]

But committing in policy and practice to the comprehensive provision of 'good' food – be it via freely available drinking water, universal school meals, community kitchens or sharing at festivities – might minimize the discriminatory character of non-market provisioning. To the extent that it also reconstitutes people as collaborative producers rather than passive consumers, it might also remove some of the alienation which has crept into our relationship with food. By enabling people (not just women!) to work more closely with the material 'stuff' of everyday life – be it through cookery classes, food-buying clubs or agro-tourism – the distance between labour and leisure can perhaps be shortened. In this sense, this is a political agenda concerned with restructuring social relations, rather than just protecting them from further commodification.

## Fair exchange

In the sphere of exchange, the rules governing international trade have come in for much criticism, although the content of those criticisms has differed. Broadly speaking, there has been a split between the advocates of free trade and those of managed trade. Those who have favoured increased levels of trade have pushed for greater liberalization of national sugar markets, locked in by legally enforceable agreements. This has been the position of many advocates of low-cost producers based in Australia, Brazil and Thailand. Those who wish to control levels of trade and defend national sovereignty have argued for greater policy-space to allow states to protect key agricultural sectors and for slower implementation of any reforms that are made. This has been the position of those connected to sugar producers in the EU, the United States and India, as well as higher-cost exporters like those in the Caribbean, African and Pacific regions that wanted to maintain their privileged access to historically protected markets.

Beyond these important but narrow debates about what constitutes a 'fair' level of border protection, a more expansive set of questions has concerned the place of sugar trade in national development strategies. Maintaining price stability for importing and exporting countries has regained popularity in the wake of world market convulsion. Some established financial traders have advanced the idea of 'circuit breakers' to suspend market trading in sugar futures at its most volatile. More ambitiously, the United Nations Conference on Trade and Development has proposed the use of counter-cyclical financing facilities to allow very poor countries to import sugar during periods of high prices and for the resurrection of commodity-specific mechanisms to support poor sugar exporters during periods of low prices.[12]

The question of how trade policy can foster economic growth has also returned, albeit in a different form. The use of infant industry protection to link sugar production to domestic refining and food manufacturing capacity has fallen out of fashion, but has been encouraged in respect of ethanol distillation and 'bio-refining' as practised in Brazil. For food sugar, the approach has been more conservative, focusing on adding value to existing exports through product upgrading, such as selling speciality sugars, such as muscovado, and functional upgrading, such as packaging sugars.

More radical proposals have sought to challenge the power held by dominant businesses in the sugar trade. These have included restricting financial speculation in global commodity markets, exposing transfer pricing by multinational sugar producers, and preventing investor-protection clauses from allowing food companies to sue governments over their public health policies. Other proposals have targeted the agro-input companies and the way seeds are exchanged. The Open Source Seed Initiative has called for an overhaul of the patenting system to allow farmers and plant breeders to save seeds and exchange germplasm in a protected commons. This means that improved varieties can be commercially traded but not privatized as such through intellectual property rights.

These efforts have also been important in shifting the political terrain. Instead of pitting one state against another as happens in the WTO, they have suggested how states in general have lost power to global capital. They have also had to politicize the opaque and complex world of business transactions, which has led to some novel forms of activism. ActionAid, for example, has offered 'tax tours' around London to explain to the public how Associated British Foods has reduced state claims on its profits by shifting earnings declarations into low-tax jurisdictions.

Another form of opposition to particular businesses in the sugar trade has been the boycott. This has long been a potent form of 'everyday' politics, going right back to the moral imperative invoked by nineteenth-century abolitionists, who suggested that by eating colonial sugar, you would also be eating the flesh of slaves. The English literature scholar Timothy Morton dubbed this the 'blood sugar' topos: a standardized way of constructing arguments about the consumption of West Indian sugar which linked it to notions of guilt and shame, especially among women.[13] This topos remains present today. As part of their Clean Sugar Campaign, Cambodian activists made a short film depicting a tin of Tate & Lyle's famous golden syrup filled with blood, evoking concern in the viewer about (their) unwitting complicity in human rights abuses.

One reason why the boycott remains popular as a political strategy is its ability to bypass the state and apply pressure directly to companies through the market, especially those sensitive to brand reputation. This can be seen in the campaigns by consumer groups and organic supporters in the United States to petition and/or boycott Coca-Cola and Kellogg's over the companies' opposition to the mandatory labelling of any genetically modified ingredients. The boycott also offers a way to register the interests of those lacking their own political voice, such as slaves or animals. To protect monkeys caught on Mauritian sugar estates and sent to the United Kingdom for animal testing, the Anti-Vivisection Coalition sought to disgrace those British companies trading Mauritian sugar and use this as leverage to have the Mauritian government acquiesce to their solution.

To the extent that boycotts offer a common-sense way to challenge trade practices, it is by portraying them in black and white: this company/product is bad, so stop giving them your money. In this respect, they are something of a blunt instrument, wielded sporadically in response to the issue of the day. A more subtle and sustained way of harnessing consumer ethics can be seen in the fair trade movement.

Initially, this relied on empathetic consumers being

willing to pay a little more for a product in the knowledge that some of this money would be channelled back to small-scale producers in the form of higher commodity prices for farmers and a premium for the community. The business of fair trade has since evolved and now flows through the major retail and manufacturing companies which it once stood in opposition to. In the case of sugar, this transition was represented by the 2008 agreement between the Fairtrade Labelling Organization (FLO) and Tate & Lyle for the latter to sell its entire UK range of direct consumption sugars under the Fairtrade label – the same Tate & Lyle also selling Cambodian sugar indirectly to consumers via food manufacturers.

This agreement has transferred around £2 million a year in premiums to the 6,000 cane farmers in Belize who had been certified by the FLO, and it has been used to pay for pest control projects and investment in social infrastructure like schools. But the scheme has had some setbacks. The producer association administering the premiums, the Belize Sugar Cane Farmers Association, has been reprimanded on numerous occasions by the FLO for financial mismanagement. There have also been complaints by farmers that they have not benefited enough in the form of higher crop prices, particularly in the context where EU reform had already lowered the market rate paid for their exports.

In asking small-scale farmers to meet exacting environmental and social demands, the FLO does not have an easy job. As well as difficulties in Belize, it has also come under pressure from the International Trades Union Congress to strip Fijian sugar of its Fairtrade status, given the rights violations during the government of military commander Frank Bainimarama (2007–2014).

Another approach to raising standards through

certification can be seen in the organization Bonsucro, which has worked with large-scale plantations as well as small-scale outgrowers. Established by a multi-stakeholder coalition including the WWF, the Brazilian milling group UNICA and brand-name companies like Bacardi, BP and Coca-Cola, the idea behind Bonsucro is to independently certify sugar-cane production against a common standard containing minimum social and environmental require-ments. Although Bonsucro certification does not bring with it any additional payment, it can help sugar producers secure long-term contracts. As mentioned in chapter 5, Coca-Cola, along with other Bonsucro members like PepsiCo and Unilever, have all made public commitments to source 100 per cent of their sugar from certified sustain-able sources by 2020.

Bonsucro has made an impressive start in penetrating the market, certifying forty-six mills and their surrounding farms in the four years since its 2011 launch.[14] This equated to 3.6 per cent of the world production of sugar cane; a pro-portion far outweighing Fairtrade, Rainforest Alliance and organic certified sugar, which collectively accounted for less than 1 per cent of world production.[15] However, ques-tions remain over the extent to which all these *voluntary* initiatives can ratchet up their existing standards and reach those producers who are far from achieving it at present. Their ability to enforce more stringent demands must be tempered by the fact that companies, ultimately, do not have to sign up to their rules.

Another concern about certification is that it creates a new locus of power in the 'audit regime' which is far removed from the daily realities of sugar production. An alternative and more accessible form of assurance for farm-ers can be found in participatory guarantee systems. These start from the premise that producers can be trusted to keep one another in check through peer review, especially where they already farm as part of a community. In 2013, pilots funded by a UN agency were under way in the Pacific islands to export organic sugar made from coconut sap using this system.[16]

This example also raises the idea of replacing industrially produced refined sugars with other sugars or sweet ingredients. These could be jaggery sugars made from cane plants and palm trees, or honey or maple syrup. As commodities amenable to artisanal production methods, they offer other opportunities for fair exchange based on local trade and direct selling, albeit in ways which require fundamental overhaul in the way that sweetness is consumed. The same line of thinking can be applied to sugar-cane biofuels. In Haiti, mechanical engineers from MIT trialled a scheme that turned crushed sugar-cane stalks into charcoal briquettes using kilns made from oil drums. This fuel was used for indoor cooking, and sought to provide an alternative to wood-derived charcoal because of the high rates of deforestation that had already taken place in the country.

A final way of re-imagining trade relations is provided by Equal Exchange, which has sister cooperatives based in the United Kingdom and the United States. These worker-owned companies have partnered with farmer-owned companies producing sugar in Paraguay, cacao in the Dominican Republic and vanilla in Madagascar to manufacture chocolate bars and other foods. These are then sold in retail outlets also sympathetic to their mission of economic democratization. In this way, Equal Exchange considers its kind of fair trade to be more authentic than that embraced by the FLO and Fair Trade USA, expanding the power of labour in alternative commodity circuits rather than rubber-stamping conventional circuits and sweeping a few crumbs down to those at the bottom. Indeed, in 2014 the farmer cooperative in Paraguay became the first in the country to own a sugar mill, building one from scratch thanks to export revenues from its Fairtrade and organic sales.[17]

## Empowered working

The approach of Equal Exchange brings us to our next vector of transformation, which concerns the empowerment of global labour. So far the book has largely discussed the disempowerment of labour by economic and political elites. According to the geographer David Harvey, these elites have done so because of the critical importance of worker compliance and cooperation to the accumulation process. Fearing strikes, inefficiencies and rising production costs, capitalists and their allies have utilized both the 'stick' of coercion and the 'carrot' of co-optation to discipline labour.[18]

Coercion can include instances of physical violence and debt bondage as we have seen, but the weapons most commonly wielded in the sugar industry have been the worsening of conditions and the threat of redundancy. To this end, efforts to end labour outsourcing have seriously weakened the capitalist armoury. By outsourcing the recruitment and management of labour to contractors, companies have been able to downgrade the legal and institutional protection afforded to workers. In Brazil, one of the inspirational moves by São Paulo's Rural Inspection Unit was to use an obscure legal directive on outsourcing to argue that, as a 'core activity', sugar-cane harvesting had to be performed in-house. This was opposed by millers and farmers who wanted to keep their labour costs and administrative burden as low as possible, but the Brazilian courts ultimately sided with the labour inspectors, allowing them to apply legal pressure on millers like Zilor who have since tried to find ways round the ruling by setting up loosely regulated shell companies.

Strategies of co-optation, meanwhile, have included the creation of quality circles and the mobilization of work pride, such as local competitions to find the fastest cane cutter or the farmer with the highest yields. These paternal forms of organization can be contrasted with more autonomous forms of organization, such as the trade union or factory council, which seek to empower workers to pursue their own interests. Although these forms of organized labour are not immune from becoming an extension of management or degenerating into corruption as we saw in chapter 4, in many instances they remain a key political force in the global sugar industry.

In Colombia, for instance, field workers stripped of additional benefits as their jobs were outsourced have formed their own union, SINALCORTEROS, to demand better contracts. This was not an easy process. After going on strike in 2005, the workers, who were predominantly black and so socially disadvantaged by skin colour too, at first sought to affiliate to an existing union at a sugar mill. They were denied precisely because they did not share the same employer. After a further strike involving thousands more cane cutters in 2008, which President Álvaro Uribe greeted with anti-riot police on the pretext that they were acting in concert with terrorist guerrillas, their union was finally recognized and they were allowed to negotiate with the mills. Although their main demand for direct employment was not met, they did gain an increase in the piece-rate payment, an end to obligatory Sunday and public holiday shifts, and extra housing allowances and sick pay.[19] Yet the hostility did not abate. In 2012, the leader of SINALCORTEROS, Daniel Aguirre, was shot dead whilst out walking with his wife; during the preceding year, another twenty-eight trade unionists in the country had been killed.[20] One thing that Aguirre had been agitating for at the time was a revision to Colombia's labour statutes to bring them into line with the ILO Conventions on freedom of association and rights to collective bargaining, which the country had already ratified more than thirty years ago.

Efforts to strengthen the sugar union movement have evolved considerably over recent decades, shaped by the ascent of neo-liberal ideology and the dismantling and discrediting of trade unions in the Global North. In the early 1980s, for instance, the International Commission for the Coordination of Solidarity Among Sugar Workers (ICCSASW), based in Canada, sought to multi-nationalize information sharing between sugar worker representatives, but the organization has since withered away. Taking its place has been the Sugar Network of the International Union of Food Workers (IUF), an international federation of trade unions which has focused its work in southern Africa. As well as changing institutional form, the union movement has changed its focus too. The IUF has moved beyond the traditional (male) concerns with wages and working conditions to tackle issues such as maternity pay and sexual harassment as well.

Other forms of labour solidarity can be found within the advocacy work of the International Trade Union Confederation, which as well as calling for a suspension of Fairtrade certification in Fiji put pressure on the EU to use its trade and aid leverage to intervene in the military government's suppression of domestic unionism. The capacity-building programmes supported by the US-based union AFL-CIO in the Colombian sugar industry and the UK-based GMB union in Guyana offer other examples of workers transcending national borders. That said, such alliances do remain rather piecemeal. It is certainly nothing to match the organization of farmers in the International Confederation of European Beet Growers, which resolutely defends their interests during EU policy negotiations in Brussels.

A more high-profile approach to defending labour, at least for observers in the Global North, has been for non-governmental organizations to act on behalf of workers and farmers via media campaigns and legal challenges. For example, the 2004 report by Human Rights Watch into child labour in El Salvador's sugar industry sharply criticized Coca-Cola for 'turning a blind eye' to the issue and called upon the company to monitor labour standards all the way down the supply chain. Some success can be claimed for these media exposés. In this case, the scrutiny helped expedite the efforts already being coordinated by the International Labour Organization and the Salvadoran Sugar Association to eradicate child labour, and, by the end of the decade, Human Rights Watch acknowledged that the numbers of children working in sugar-cane agriculture had fallen considerably. But by the same token they also questioned the extent to which these children had been integrated into the education system or had been simply left to fend for themselves, a result put down to the absence of a domestic grassroots movement advocating children's rights more widely.[21]

Another case of transnational activism can be seen in Nicaragua, where communities of sugar-cane workers and their families established the association ASOCHIVIDA to protest at an epidemic of chronic kidney disease, which killed an estimated three thousand workers in their community between 1997 and 2007.[22] The explanation for this epidemic has been controversial. Locals argued that it was due to the working conditions of the sugar industry, including acute dehydration and exposure to agro-chemicals. The industry replied that the scientific evidence was inconclusive and noted that workers in other parts of Nicaragua suffered from this disease too. Seeking to move beyond this impasse, ASOCHIVIDA teamed up with the Center for International Environmental Law to file a complaint against the World Bank's International Finance Corporation for lending millions of dollars to National Sugar Estates Limited, Nicaragua's biggest sugar producer and employer of the association's workers. This triggered a dialogue between the two parties which resulted in a study into the causes of the disease and donations of food aid and some medical provision by the company.

The initial findings of the study, carried out by researchers from Boston University, demurred on whether dehydration and chemical exposure were causes of the disease. A charity founded in 2008 by an American filmmaker and a former Nicaraguan cane cutter explicitly to address this issue has been more forthright. La Isla Foundation has used those familiar boomerang tactics of western media coverage and organizational alliance (with Fairfood International and Solidaridad in the Netherlands) to make the case that working conditions *have* been a contributory cause of the disease. For them, it was not just basic occupational health that was needed, such as giving field workers regular water, rest and shade. Rather, the more fundamental issue was one of empowerment, whereby the right to associate, to access judicial mechanisms and to be free from intimidation were all essential for tackling the social determinants of this hitherto unknown form of chronic kidney disease.[23]

This criticism of national-level legal failings has been raised already, the large numbers of cases brought to the

International Labour Organization about the widespread violation of the right to associate being a case in point. But another way in which the voices of workers and farmers have been amplified has been through reform of industry-level institutions. In the run-up to the amendment of Kenya's Sugar Act in 2011, for example, the Kenya Human Rights Commission put forward a list of recommendations to improve the livelihoods of sugar-cane farmers. These focused on the importance of decision-making processes in the industry being intelligible, accessible and contestable. They included recommendations to (a) restructure the Kenya Sugar Board to better represent farmers; (b) decentralize Sugar Arbitration Tribunal hearings from the capital Nairobi to the sugar-growing regions so they could be better attended; (c) have independent agencies manage the cane-weighing process which determines how much farmers are paid; and (d) enable the Land Control Board to intervene in land transactions to make sure that women are not excluded when farm ownership changes hands. Similar calls have been made by the Fairtrade Foundation to include smallholders within the governing structures of national public–private agricultural schemes being rolled out in Africa.

Ultimately, of course, empowerment has to come from within so, as important as such institutional changes are, they must also resonate with a sense within labourers themselves that they can transform their own working lives. This chimes with the point made earlier about Caribbean workers renouncing their dehumanizing identities of 'nigger' and 'coolie' during the region's independence movement. One process by which this is supported today is through techniques which recognize labourers *as* agents. For instance, the geographer Pamela Ngwenya-Richardson has used participatory video techniques to capture the experience of workers and farmers in the Barbados sugar industry from their point of view. Not only did this highlight the powerful emotional attachments that they had to their work, it also led to important questions being asked of officials when the documentary was screened at a community meeting. Magazine articles celebrating the renegade organic cane farmer Leontino Balbo Junior, public talks by female union leaders like Alfamir Castillo, and even museum exhibitions retelling the stories of freedom-fighting sugar slaves have also helped labourers to narrate their own stories and highlight their capacity to transform their circumstances.

A final point on empowered working relates to technology. We noted previously the persuasive appeal of 'modernization' in its current incarnation of mechanized harvesting, precision farming and factory diversification. Even if labour is better represented in terms of industry decision making or ownership, it is questionable how much will change if jobs still disappear and the work is still alienating. Although it has fallen out of fashion now, there is much to be salvaged from literature of the mid-twentieth century on appropriate technology. This was associated with the work of economist E. F. Schumacher. His philosophy was that capital-intensive technology, developed in the industrialized countries of the West, was not appropriate for the world's predominantly agrarian countries and that labour-intensive, small-scale and locally controlled technologies should be adopted instead. Applied to sugar production, this led to tangible changes in the way the industry developed, encouraging support for jaggery sugars made via open-pan crystallization in countries like India and Kenya. A study by the UN agency UNIDO in the late 1970s argued that while it would take twenty of these units to make the same sugar as one vacuum-pan sugar factory, it would cost less to build and employ five times as many people.

Although development agencies and government planners are less attracted to such 'appropriate technology' than they once were, research on the topic has persisted. Some of this is grouped together by Panela Monitor, a website set up by a Venezuelan company to build market supply and demand for jaggery sugar (called *panela* in Latin America). Another approach has been taken by researchers at the Federal Rural University of Pernambuco in Brazil, who have been developing mechanical harvesters that can be worn by field workers. The intention of these is to reduce the intensity of cane cutting, avoid worker unemployment and allow cane to be harvested in hilly areas and without soil compaction. Lastly, agro-ecological farming has been promoted in various guises around the world. This challenges the reliance on genetically modified crops and agro-chemical applications delivered by input companies by promoting on-farm innovation and knowledge-intensive agricultural practices instead. In short, it is about using technology that allows farmers to work with nature rather than against it, and leads us nicely on to the final demand.

## Diverse land

As argued by the geographer Tony Weis, the aim of moving agricultural systems off the chemical and fossil energy treadmill and onto a lower-input and more biodiverse pathway is not about going backwards to more 'primitive' approaches.[24] On the contrary, cutting-edge science exploring the functional complementarities of different plant and animal species has been used to inform biological pest and disease control techniques. Likewise, research into nutrient recycling and retention has been used to build up soil fertility through the use of specific crop rotations and green manures. Where agro-ecology does depart from conventional agriculture is in making farmers key participants in the process of innovation, valuing the wisdom they have accrued through generations of experimental, observational and working knowledge rather than dismissing it. In this sense, we can think of it as a de-colonial endeavour for epistemic justice, in which people dominated by the ideas of western metropolitan elites demand that their worldviews be recognized as valid forms of knowledge.

Within sugar-cane and sugar-beet agriculture, patches of agro-ecological practice can be seen right around the world. In Uttar Pradesh, the state government has promoted inter-cropping, which involves cultivating sugar cane alongside crops such as potato, mustard and garlic. While this reduces the tonnage of sugar cane harvested because it cannot be planted as intensively, growing short-duration crops does have the advantage of providing farmers with additional income prior to the sugar-cane harvest. Meanwhile, in Guyana, the national sugar company GuySuCo has moved to phase out all pesticide spraying on its estates and instead control pests through the release of natural predators raised in its insectaries and through the targeted flooding of fields. Finally, in the Philippines, after being given control of a sugar-cane plantation, the Flora community experimented with the use of green manure. This involved chopping the leaves off the sugar-cane plant a few months before its harvest and allowing them to decompose on the soil, thereby increasing the amount of nitrogen and organic matter in the land and reducing the amount of fertilizer needed.[25]

In some cases, sugar farmers have avoided *all* forms of chemical fertilizer and pesticides in order to go organic. Sold under 'certified organic' labels, this type of sugar has become increasingly popular with consumers. According to the International Sugar Organization, worldwide sales grew from around 30,000 tonnes in 1999 to 300,000 tonnes in 2009, although as noted previously this only comprised a tiny fraction of total sugar consumed.[26]

Around a third of this market is supplied by the Brazilian farmer mentioned previously, Leontino Balbo Junior. Balbo's story is an interesting one. For years, he worked against the grain of scientific consensus in the industry, using the green manure technique by chopping off the leaves mechanically with a specially designed harvester, which also had softened tyres to reduce soil compaction. He then began to spray the vinasse left over from the milling process back onto the fields instead of fertilizer, and relied on insectaries and the now ecologically rich fields to produce the natural predators needed to control pests. None of this came quickly, taking almost three decades to establish as an integrated system. Nor was it straightforward. Yields first declined before they improved, and there was tension with the estate workers who wanted cane burning to continue so they could carry on earning wages through manual harvesting. Nevertheless, Balbo has successfully demonstrated that holistic agro-ecology – what he calls 'ecosystem revitalising agriculture' – can prosper in one of the most competitive sugar and ethanol markets in the world.[27]

Dissociating agro-ecological practices from romantic notions of traditional peasant farming is important because they can be integrated into industrial agriculture. A recent example is provided in the American sugar-beet industry. In the 2010s, the Department of Agriculture investigated how to reduce fertilizer and pesticide use through better crop rotation. Agronomists in the Department concluded that, by lengthening and diversifying the rotation – planting sugar beet one season, then barley and then nitrogen-fixing soybean – both soil fertility and plant health could be improved. In addition, some sugar-beet farmers in the state of Montana have begun to practise no-till agriculture, which means that, rather than ploughing up the land after harvest, they leave the plant stubble in the field to protect the soil from erosion.

For critics of industrial agriculture like ecologist Miguel Altieri, however, these selective attempts to reduce dependence on agro-chemicals do not constitute a *genuine* agro-ecological approach. For example, both crop rotation and no-till agriculture have been used on large-scale land-holdings in conjunction with mechanized farming, GM seeds and powerful herbicides (albeit in reduced quantities). For Altieri, agro-ecology is about embracing principles such as species and genetic diversity at both the field and landscape levels – a principle which is fundamentally incompatible with this kind of monoculture production.[28]

An example of this incompatibility is the introduction of the cane toad to Queensland in the 1930s. Meant to be a quick external fix for the sugar industry's pest problem, the toad, which was not native to the country, turned out to be an ecological disaster. It failed to eat the insects laying the harmful larvae and instead devoured other fauna and poisoned larger animals with its toxic skin. As its population exploded, the cane toad was reclassified as an invasive species and the Australian government now spends millions of dollars each year trying to control its spread.

This takes us to the other way in which the demand for diverse land can be understood. What I have described so far are changes to the cultivation of sugar crops that in some way improve their environmental profile. But for most figures in the agro-ecology movement, the very production of export-oriented and inedible cash crops like sugar cane is considered problematic. They believe that agriculture as a whole must be reoriented towards the production of staple foods by small-scale farmers. This is about the diversity of what is grown *and* who grows it.

The flagship case here is Cuba. As discussed in chapter 3, when the Soviet Union imploded in the late 1980s, Cuban sugar exports went with it. Worse still, without foreign exchange to pay for oil and fertilizers, the entire agricultural sector began to collapse. It has been estimated that, by the early 1990s, average daily calorific and protein intake across the country had fallen by almost a third.[29] This crisis prompted smallholders, known as *campesinos*, to revert to low-input farming, using compost and draught power instead of fertilizers and tractors. Meanwhile, the Cuban government began to break up the collectivized farms and turn over sugar plantations to cooperatives made up of former workers.

Like Balbo's agro-ecology in Brazil, it took time for the cooperatives to adjust to running their own farms, but, by the end of the decade, and supported by nascent urban gardening enterprises that had sprung up, the chronic food shortages of the early 1990s had all but disappeared. Cuba has since become a flagship for the argument that poor countries can de-link themselves from international trade and industrial agriculture. Not everyone is convinced. Some point out that, although Cuba trades less, its agricultural balance has swung such that it is now a net food importer, a deficit which is likely to grow further as trade relations with the United States normalize.[30] Nevertheless, for people like Peter Rosset, the country's experience shows that the adoption of agro-ecological technology, alongside agrarian reform and protection against food dumping, can create a preferable alternative to the way that the agrarian economy is currently organized. This alternative is known as food sovereignty.[31]

Food sovereignty is not about self-sufficiency for countries, then, but autonomy for producers. Since the 1990s it has been a rallying call of rural organizations across the Global South, many of which are members of the global peasant alliance La Via Campesina. One of these members is the Movimento dos Trabalhadores Rurais Sem Terra (MST), translated as the Landless Rural Workers' Movement. Based in Brazil, the organization's history is closely bound with sugar cane, tracing its ideological roots to the *quilombos* communities of runaway sugar slaves and the Peasant League societies that sprang from the waged sugar-cane workers in the north-east of the country.

The aim of the MST has been to settle landless workers on land, and to achieve this it has organized occupations. These have brought it into direct conflict with the sugar-cane industry. In 2006, in the state of Minas Gerais, around a thousand MST families began using water to grow fruit and vegetables from a canal bound for sugar-cane fields before being evicted, while the following year hundreds of MST members (mainly women) held sit-ins on the grounds of the Cevesa mill in São Paulo in protest against the expansion of what to them was an alien (and alienating) form of agriculture.[32]

The MST has justified its approach with reference to the country's constitutional ruling on agrarian reform, which holds that only rural property that is not performing its 'social function' should be expropriated. They take this to mean that land should provide jobs and improve living standards, and so have demanded the occupation of unproductive farms and a halt to the expansion of capital-intensive sugar-cane and soybean farms.

The MST now claims to have 350,000 families in long-term, legally recognized settlements with another 90,000 members living precariously in camps on contested property.[33] This has been a bloody struggle. In what has become a depressing theme in this book, a leader of the MST, Cicero Guedes, was shot dead in 2013. The assassination happened outside a disused sugar plantation in the state of Rio de Janeiro which had been occupied by the MST as they tried to expedite its legal redistribution.

Compared to the experience of Cuba, which was conditioned by enforced economic crisis and managed by a government immune from electoral pressure, agrarian reform in Brazil has been far more piecemeal. This reminds us of the importance of context and the different directions that land reform can take. For instance, following the end of Apartheid in South Africa in 1994, the main issue there has not been taking farmland *out* of sugarcane production but of *transferring it to* the previously disenfranchised black population. Around 21 per cent of cane land held by white growers has now been sold to black growers, short of the 30 per cent target set for 2014 and with additional concerns being raised about the lack of support for new owners once they move onto the farms.[34]

Part of the reason for the shortfall was the difficulty of basing land redistribution on voluntary market transactions. This was known as the willing buyer–willing seller model and was being popularized by the World Bank at the time. But in South Africa, government grants for potential buyers proved too small and the interest among potential sellers too low. Efforts to accelerate the process since have hit a number of roadblocks, not least the understandable reluctance of existing farmers to have their land expropriated without significant compensation. To this end, the country's largest independent cane farmer, Charl Senekal, has said that any attempts to facilitate the sale of land below market price should not be entertained: 'It is enshrined in our Constitution that we will be paid a market value rate for our land.'[35]

In Trinidad, meanwhile, the land question has been how to redistribute state-owned sugar-cane farms that have been left fallow. In 2014, twelve years after the industry's closure, former sugar workers and farmers were still petitioning the government to expedite the transfer of land to them as initially promised, rather than prepare it for private investors as now appeared to be happening.[36] And in another example from Ecuador, it has been the control of irrigated water by the sugar industry and other agribusiness that has been targeted for reform. Groups from the mestizo, indigenous and Afro-Ecuadorian population have mobilized around the demand for the right to water to be included in the government's 2008 constitutional amendment and for the creation of a Plurinational Council on Water so that they can participate in the decisions affecting water provision.[37]

In each of these countries, then, the relationship between sugar production and agrarian reform has differed, as have the social alliances agitating for change. That said, in thinking about the possibilities for 'reform from below', the MST offers a number of insights relevant to these varied struggles for land redistribution and equitable resource management.

First is the way it has challenged assumptions about how land should be used. We saw in chapter 5 how large-scale land acquisitions have been justified by investors on the basis that the land in question is being under-utilized because it is not dedicated to intensive monoculture production. What the MST has done is to raise the question of whether this is a legitimate way to utilize land if it does not create sufficient waged employment and fails to prevent the depletion and degradation of its surrounding environment.

Second, it has demonstrated ways of working both with

and against the state. As articulated by the sociologist Wendy Wolford, the movement has presented itself to the rural populace as a means of negotiating with an otherwise corrupt and predatory state. Its ambition has not been to replace the state, but rather to work through it, cajoling its leaders into making the rule of law compatible with greater territorial autonomy.[38]

Finally, it has shown how the tensions between opponents of industrial agriculture and those rural labourers that depend on it for wages can be navigated. The concept of *sem terra* (landlessness) has served to forge a connection between these two groups based not on their different livelihoods but on their shared experiences of poverty and exploitation, later cemented with collective cultural experiences like marches and music. This shows that attention to the political sociology of resistance is all important if counter-hegemonic projects like food sovereignty are to take root both within and beyond the Global South.

## Conclusion

Looking back over this chapter, we have seen a variety of ways in which people have tried to make sugar provisioning more ecologically sound and socially just. Such pluralism is to be championed. There is no single, universal way to transform the production, exchange and consumption of sugar for the better, and we should be sceptical of anyone who proposes such a feat. At the same time, transformation does remain necessary. Let us remind ourselves of the interlocking problems facing the global populace. There are hundreds of millions of people going chronically hungry and unable to access land and the same number of people suffering illness and premature death linked to obesity and diabetes. There are also tens of millions of people unable to scratch out a decent living as workers or farmers in the sugar industry.

For some, the answers to these challenges are to be found in technical modifications. Adding vitamins to sugar, lowering the calorie content of food, boosting crop yields or reducing water intensity all seem to promise immediate and painless solutions. This book has cautioned against such commodity fetishism. Progressive change will not come from changing our relationship to sugar but only from changing our relationships to one another. That is both the challenge and the potential of the politics of sugar, and, indeed, of capitalism itself.

# Notes

I INTRODUCTION

1 FAO (2013), *The State of Food and Agriculture*, Rome: FAO, p. ix.
2 There is no material shortage of food that would account for high levels of hunger. FAO data shows a steady increase in the global supply of per capita calories from primary crops, from an average availability of 2,193 calories per day in 1961 to 2,868 in 2011. Retrieved 28 October 2014 from http://faostat3.fao.org/download/FB/FBS/E
3 Sergey Gudoshnikov, Jolly Lindsay and Donald Spence (2004), *The World Sugar Market*, London: CRC Press.
4 J. Steele, J. Shen, G. Tsakos, E. Fuller, S. Morris, R. Watt, C. Guarnizo-Herreño and J. Wildman (2014), 'The Interplay between Socioeconomic Inequalities and Clinical Oral Health', *Journal of Dental Research*, OnlineFirst doi: 10.1177/0022034514553978.
5 IBIS World (2014), *Global Sugar Manufacturing Market Research Report*. Retrieved 11 February 2015 from http://www.ibisworld.com/industry/global/global-sugar-manufacturing.html
6 World Bank (2007), *World Development Report 2008: Agriculture for Development*, Washington, DC: World Bank, p. 99.
7 Roger Thurow and Geoff Winestock (2002), 'Addiction to Sugar Subsidies Chokes Poor Nations' Exports', *Wall Street Journal*, Leader, 16 September 2002.
8 Figures on operating profits or net earnings are taken from company's respective annual reports, excepting Mars which does not publish such figures.
9 Robert Lustig, *Fat Chance: The Hidden Truth about Sugar, Obesity and Disease* (2013), New York: Hudson Street Press; Jeff O'Connell (2010), *Sugar Nation: The Hidden Truth Behind*

*America's Deadliest Habit and the Simple Way to Beat It*, New York: Hyperion; Michael Moss (2013), *Salt, Sugar, Fat*, New York and London: Random House.

10  OECD-FAO (2014), *OECD-FAO Agricultural Outlook 2014–2023*, Paris: OECD Publishing, p. 162.

11  Michael Moss (2013), *Salt, Sugar, Fat*, New York, London: Random House, p. 347.

12  Andrew Gamble (1999) 'Marxism after Communism', *Review of International Studies* 25(2): 127–44.

13  For detail on crop determinism, see Barry Higman (2000), 'The Sugar Revolution', *The Economic History Review* 53(2): 213–36.

14  Grace Nichols (1983) *I is a Long Memoried Woman*, London: Karnak House, pp. 32–5.

15  Elizabeth Abbott (2009), *Sugar: A Bittersweet History*, London and New York: Duckworth Overlook.

16  Jack Galloway (2000), 'Sugar', in Kenneth Kiple and Kriemhild Coneè Ornelas (eds), *The Cambridge World History of Food*, Cambridge: Cambridge University Press, pp. 437–49.

17  Adam Snowdon (2012), 'Why a Fat Tax would be a Terrible Idea', Adam Smith Institute Blog, 15 May 2012. Retrieved 28 October 2014 from http://www.adamsmith.org/blog/tax-spending/why-a-fat-tax-would-be-a-terrible-idea/

18  Adam Smith (2006 [1776]), *An Inquiry into the Nature and Causes of the Wealth of Nations*, University Park: The Pennsylvania State University Press, p. 775.

19  David Eltis (2001), 'The Volume and Structure of the Transatlantic Slave Trade: A Reassessment', *The William and Mary Quarterly* 58(1): 17–46.

20  Leigh Day (2014), 'CARICOM Nations Unanimously Approve 10 Point Plan for Slavery Reparations', Leigh Day News, 11 March 2014. Retrieved 28 October 2014 from http://www.leighday.co.uk/News/2014/March-2014/CARICOM-nations-unanimously-approve-10-point-plan

21  Ulbe Bosma (2013), *The Sugar Plantation in India and Indonesia: Industrial Production, 1770–2010*, Cambridge: Cambridge University Press.

22  Seymour Drescher (2007), 'Women's Mobilization in the Era of Slave Emancipation: Some Anglo-French Comparisons', in Kathryn Kish Sklar and James Brewer Stewart (eds), *Women's*

Rights and Transatlantic Antislavery in the Era of Emancipation,
New Haven, CT: Yale University Press, pp. 98–120.
23 Michael Niblett (2012), 'World-Economy, World-Ecology, World-
Literature', *Green Letters: Studies in Ecocriticism* 16(1): 15–30.
24 Frères des Hommes (2007), 'Brazil: Defending Small-Scale
Agriculture Against Industrial Farming', Frères des Hommes
web page, 17 April 2007. Retrieved 28 October 2014 from
http://fdh.org/Brazil-Defending-small-scale.html#nb2

## 2 GROWING MARKETS, GROWING WAISTLINES

1 Retrieved 28 October 2014 from http://faostat3.fao.org/
download/Q/QD/E
2 Michael Moss (2013), *Salt, Sugar, Fat*, New York, London:
Random House, p. 55.
3 See Jennie Macdiarmid and John Blundell (1998), 'Assessing
Dietary Intake: Who, What and Why of Under-Reporting',
*Nutrition Research Reviews* 11(2): 231–53.
4 Anne Marie Thow and Corinna Hawkes (2009), 'The
Implications of Trade Liberalization for Diet and Health: A Case
Study from Central America', *Globalization and Health* 5(5): 2.
5 Barry Popkin (2006), 'Global Nutrition Dynamics: The World is
Shifting Rapidly Toward a Diet Linked with Noncommunicable
Diseases', *The American Journal of Clinical Nutrition* 84(2): 294.
6 Frost and Sullivan* (2012), 'Assessment of the Intelligent
Vending Machines Market', Intel Corporation Report,
November 2011, no page numbers. Retrieved 28 October 2014
from http://www.intel.co.uk/content/dam/www/public/us/en/
documents/white-papers/retail-intelligent-vending-white-
paper.pdf
7 A slotting fee is a fee paid by manufacturers to retailers to
have their product placed in store. Higher-profile retail spots
command higher fees.
8 This must be qualified, particularly in the Indian context where
*gur* and *khandasari* (non-industrial refined sugar) remain
popular. Their appeal to producers has been attributed to the
higher prices offered by non-traditional processors vis-à-vis
industrial mills, and their appeal to consumers due to the
sugar's supposed health benefits and the fact that it contains

molasses from which illicit liquor can be distilled.

9  Gary Taubes and Cristen Kearns Couzens (2012), 'Big Sugar's Sweet Little Lies', *Mother Jones*, November/December 2012. Retrieved 24 March 2015 from http://www.motherjones.com/ environment/2012/10/sugar-industry-lies-campaign

10  Ben Fine, Michael Heasman and Judith Wright (1996), *Consumption in the Age of Affluence: The World of Food*, London: Routledge.

11  The Coca-Cola Company (2013) 2013 Annual Review, p. 26. Retrieved 28 October 2014 from http://www.coca-colacompany. com/annual-review/2013/img/TCCC_2013_Annual_Review.pdf

12  In 2011, Coca-Cola bottlers bought an estimated 8 per cent of the world's supply of industrial-use sugar.

13  F. O. Licht (2013), *International Sugar and Sweetener Report* 146(4): 35–6.

14  See Adam Drewnowski (2003), 'Fat and Sugar: An Economic Analysis', *The Journal of Nutrition* 133(3): 838S–405S; and Barry Popkin and Samara Joy Nielson (2003), 'The Sweetening of the World's Diet', *Obesity Research* 11(11): 1325–32.

15  Marion Nestle (2002), *Food Politics: How the Food Industry Influences Nutrition and Health*, Berkeley and Los Angeles, CA: University of California Press; Consumers International (no date), The Junk Food Generation: A Multi-Country Survey of the Influence of Television Advertisements on Children, Consumers International report. Retrieved 28 October 2014 from http://epsl. asu.edu/ceru/Articles/CERU-0407-227-OWI.pdf

16  Sandra Calvert (2008), 'Children as Consumers: Advertising and Marketing', *The Future of Children* 18(1): 205–34.

17  Yuhua Guo (2000), 'Family Relations: The Generation Gap at the Table', in Jun Jing (ed.), *Feeding China's Little Emperors: Food, Children and Social Change*. Stanford, CA: Stanford University Press, pp. 94–113; Terrence Witkowski (2007), 'Food Marketing and Obesity in Developing Countries: Analysis, Ethics, and Public Policy', *Journal of Macromarketing* 27(2): 126–37.

18  Coca-Cola (2008), *Annual Review, 2007*, Atlanta: Coca-Cola Company.

19  UK National Statistics (2013), *Family Food 2012*, London: Department for Environment, Food and Rural Affairs.

20  Barry Popkin (1993), 'Nutritional Patterns and Transitions', *Population and Development Review* 19(1): 138–57.

21  Laura Schmidt (2014), 'New Unsweetened Truths about Sugar',
    *Journal of the American Medical Association (JAMA) Internal
    Medicine* 174(4): 525–6; UK National Statistics (2013), *Family
    Food 2012*, London: Department for Environment, Food and
    Rural Affairs, p. 43.
22  http://adage.com/article/the-big-tent/soft-drink-industry-smart-
    target-hispanics-blacks/235407/
23  Marco Caliendo and Wang-Sheng Lee (2013), 'Fat Chance!
    Obesity and the Transition from Unemployment to
    Employment', *Economics and Human Biology* 11(2): 121–33.
24  World Health Organization (2014), Global Health Observatory:
    Noncommunicable Diseases web page. Retrieved 28 October
    2014 from http://www.who.int/gho/ncd/en/
25  Menaka Rao (2014), 'How to Live and Die on the New Dharavi
    Diet', *Grist Media*, 29 October 2014.
26  John Yudkin (1972), *Pure, White and Deadly: How Sugar is Killing
    Us and What We Can Do to Stop It*, London: Davis-Poynter.
27  Robert Lustig (2013), *Fat Chance: The Hidden Truth about Sugar,
    Obesity and Disease*, New York: Hudson Street Press.
28  Simonette Te Morenga, Lisa Mallard and Jim Mann (2013),
    'Dietary Sugars and Body Weight: Systematic Review and Meta-
    Analyses of Randomised Controlled Trials and Cohort Studies',
    *British Medical Journal* 346: e7492.
29  Sanjay Basu, Paula Yoffe, Nancy Hills and Robert Lustig
    (2013), 'The Relationship of Sugar to Population-Level Diabetes
    Prevalence: An Econometric Analysis of Repeated Cross-
    Sectional Data', *PLoS One* 8(2): e57873.
30  Taubes and Kearns Couzens (2012), 'Big Sugar's Sweet Little
    Lies'.
31  Felicity Lawrence (2008), *Eat Your Heart Out: Why the Food
    Business is Bad for the Planet and Your Health*, London: Penguin
    Books.
32  Nestle, *Food Politics: How the Food Industry Influences Nutrition
    and Health*.
33  Miranda Prynne (2014), 'Tooth Decay is the Biggest Cause
    of Primary School Children Being Hospitalised', *The Daily
    Telegraph*, 13 July 2014. Retrieved 28 October 2014 from http://
    www.telegraph.co.uk/health/healthnews/10964323/Tooth-
    decay-is-the-biggest-cause-of-primary-school-children-being-
    hospitalised.html

34 Consensus Action on Salt and Health (2014), 'Worldwide Experts Unite to Reverse Obesity Epidemic by Forming "Action on Sugar"', Consensus Action on Salt and Health Press Release, 9 January 2014. Retrieved 28 October 2014 from http://www. actiononsalt.org.uk/actiononsugar/Press%20Release%20/ 120017.html

35 European Commission (2012), *Diabesity: A World-Wide Challenge*, Brussels: European Commission, p. 6.

36 Rob Moodie, David Stuckler, Carlos Monteiro, Nick Sheron, Bruce Neal, Thaksaphon Thamarangsi, Paul Lincoln and Sally Casswell (2013), 'Profits and Pandemics: Prevention of Harmful Effects of Tobacco, Alcohol, and Ultra-Processed Food and Drink Industries', *The Lancet* 381(9867): 670–9.

37 Amy Guthrie (2014), 'Survey Shows Mexicans Drinking Less Soda After Tax', *Wall Street Journal*, 3 October 2014.

38 The Coca-Cola Company (2014), United States Securities and Exchange Commission Form 10-K, p. 11. Retrieved 9 February 2015 from http://assets.coca-colacompany.com/do/c1/7afc6e69 49c8adf1168a3328b2ad/2013-annual-report-on-form-10-k.pdf

39 Scheherazade Daneshkhu (2014), 'Drastic Measures', *The Financial Times*, 25 April 2014, p. 9.

40 P. A. Smeets, C. de Graaf, A. Stafleu, M. J. van Osch and J. van der Grond (2005), 'Functional Magnetic Resonance Imaging of Human Hypothalamic Responses to Sweet Taste and Calories', *American Journal of Clinical Nutrition* 82(5): 1011–16.

41 Qing Yang (2010), 'Gain Weight by "Going Diet"? Artificial Sweeteners and the Neurobiology of Sugar Cravings', *Yale Journal of Biology and Medicine* 83(2): 101–8. Italics added.

42 This is sugar coated in polyphenols, which makes it more resistant to digestion and thus provides a lower sucrose 'spike' when eaten.

43 Gyorgy Scrinis (2013), *Nutritionism: The Science and Politics of Dietary Advice*, New York: Columbia University Press.

44 Editors (2013 [1913]), 'JAMA 100 Years Ago: Sugar as Food', *Journal of the American Medical Association* 310(7): 752.

45 House of Commons Environmental Audit Committee (2008), *Are Biofuels Sustainable? First Report of Session 2007–08*, London: The Stationery Office Limited, p. 24.

46 Richard Pike (2014), 'Response to Chief Medical Officer Comments on the Possibility of a Sugar Tax', British Sugar

Press Release, 6 March 2014. Retrieved 28 October 2014 from http://www.britishsugar.co.uk/Media/2014/Response-to-Chief-Medical-Officer-comments-on-the-.aspx

47  The Cuban 'food basket' has been steadily phased out from 2010.

## 3  TERMINAL TRADE DEPENDENCY

1  Data sourced from FAOSTAT.

2  Ben Richardson (2009), *Sugar: Refined Power in a Global Regime*. Basingstoke: Palgrave Macmillan, p. 89.

3  Donald Larson and Brent Borrell (2001), 'Sugar Policy and Reform', World Bank Policy Research Working Paper, April 2001, p. 6. Retrieved 28 October 2014 from http://elibrary. worldbank.org/doi/pdf/10.1596/1813-9450-2602

4  United States Department of Agriculture (USDA) Foreign Agricultural Service (2013), 'Brazil: Sugar Annual Report', USDA Global Agricultural Information Network Report, 22 April 2013. Retrieved 28 October 2014 from http://gain. fas.usda.gov/Recent%20GAIN%20Publications/SUGAR%20 ANNUAL_Sao%20Paulo%20ATO_Brazil_4-22-2013.pdf

5  Isis Almeida and Lucia Kassai (2013), 'Brazil Crushing Sugar to Ethanol with Caps on Fuel Prices', *Bloomberg News*, 19 December 2013. Retrieved 28 October 2014 from http:// www.bloomberg.com/news/2013-12-19/brazil-crushing-sugar-to-ethanol-with-caps-on-fuel-prices.html

6  UNICA (2014), 'In the Middle of the Greatest Crisis in their History, Sugarcane Producers Await the Finalization of Public Policies that Will Benefit the Sector', UNICA News, 18 December 2014. Retrieved 2 February 2015 from http://www. unica.com.br/news/3747562592033266204/in-the-middle-of-the-greatest-crisis-in-their-history-por-cento2C-sugarcane-producers-await-the-finalization-of-public-policies-that-will-benefit-the-sector/

7  Alonso Soto (2014), 'Brazil to Give Tax Benefits to Sugar, Ethanol Producers – Source', *Reuters News*, 10 September 2014. Retrieved 2 February 2015 from http://af.reuters.com/article/ energyOilNews/idAFL1N0RB0GA20140910

8  In 2001, the EU was given a waiver for its non-reciprocal trade

agreements with the ACP countries, thanks to trade concessions towards Thailand, Indonesia and the Philippines over canned tuna and towards Latin America over bananas.

9  Rural Payments Agency (2014), 'RPA Announces 2014 SPS Entitlement Values', Press Release, 20 November 2014. Retrieved 25 March 2015 from https://www.gov.uk/government/news/rpa-announces-2014-sps-entitlement-values

10  This income support is not exclusively for sugar production since beet is grown in rotation with other crops like wheat and barley. Average farm size calculated by author from 'CEFS Sugar Statistics 2014' web page. Retrieved 25 March 2015 from http://www.comitesucre.org/site/wp-content/uploads/2015/03/CEFS-SUGAR-STATISTICS-2014.pdf

11  ActionAid (2013), 'ActionAid Exposes Tax Avoidance by Associated British Food Group in Zambia', ActionAid News, 14 February 2013. Retrieved 13 January 2015 from http://www.actionaid.org.uk/news-and-views/actionaid-exposes-tax-avoidance-by-associated-british-food-group-in-zambia

12  BBC (2005), 'EU Agrees Cut in Sugar Subsidies', BBC News, 24 November 2005. Retrieved 13 January 2015 from http://news.bbc.co.uk/1/hi/business/4466388.stm

13  Czarnikow (2013), 'Why a Depressed Price is Just Not Fair Value', Czarnikow News, 21 October 2013. Retrieved 28 October 2014 from http://www.czarnikow.com/news/21/10/13/why-depressed-price-just-not-fair-value

14  Retrieved 16 February 2015 from http://en.mercopress.com/2011/07/07/sweet-sugar-hikes-fao-food-price-index-in-june-to-39-above-a-year-ago

15  OCED-FAO (2012), OECD-FAO Agricultural Outlook 2012–2021, Paris: OECD, p. 116.

16  The residual nature refers to the small proportion of overall production which passes through the world market, meaning that sudden purchases, such as those made by the USSR and the United States during this time, would have a disproportionately large effect on price.

17  The large sunk costs mean that sugar continues to be produced even at low prices because of the difficulty in changing fixed capital to produce something else.

18  Shaun Breslin (2013), 'China and the South: Objectives, Actors and Interactions', Development and Change 44(6): 1273–94.

19  People's Republic of China Ministry of Commerce (2013), 'Regular Press Conference of the Ministry of Commerce on June 18, 2013', Ministry of Commerce News, 18 June 2013. Retrieved 28 October 2014 from http://english.mofcom.gov.cn/article/newsrelease/press/201306/20130600180374.shtml

20  Raúl Prebisch (1950), *The Economic Development of Latin America and its Principal Problems*. UN document E/CN, 12/89/Rev. 1, New York: United Nations.

21  Sebastian Balfour (1990), *Castro*, Harlow: Pearson Education, p. 47.

22  Cited in Brian Pollitt (2004), 'The Rise and Fall of the Cuban Sugar Economy', *Journal of Latin American Studies* 36(2): 319–48.

23  Jorge Pérez-López (1991), *The Economics of Cuban Sugar*, Pittsburgh: University of Pittsburgh Press.

24  Another state strategy to bypass the world market has been to conduct barter exchange instead, as when Brazil swapped sugar for Nigerian oil during the 1970s.

25  Michael Fakhri (2014), *Sugar and the Making of International Trade Law*, Cambridge: Cambridge University Press.

26  Larson and Borrell (2001), 'Sugar Policy and Reform'.

27  During the twentieth century, the major world exchanges for sugar were the New York Board of Trade (NYBOT) and the London International Financial Futures and Options Exchange (LIFFE). Both have now been acquired by the US-based Intercontinental Exchange, in deals worth US$1 billion and US$8.2 billion, respectively.

28  Data retrieved 16 February 2015 from http://www.futuresindustry.org/files/css/magazineArticles/article-1383.pdf

29  Retrieved 16 February 2015 from https://www.youtube.com/watch?v=Gawo63E18jQ

30  Javier Blas (2011), 'High Speed Trading Blamed for Sugar Rises', *The Financial Times*, 8 February 2011.

31  Gina Chon (2014), 'Exchanges Urge Overhaul of Trading Rules', *The Financial Times*, 8 July 2014.

32  Institute for Agriculture and Trade Policy (2007), 'US, EU Block Brazilian Attempt to Slash Biofuel Tariffs at WTO', IATP News, 5 November 2007. Retrieved 13 January 2015 from http://www.iatp.org/news/us-eu-block-brazilian-attempt-to-slash-biofuel-tariffs-at-wto

33  United States Department of Agriculture (USDA) Economic
    Research Service (2014), Sugar and Sweeteners Yearbook Tables
    web page. Retrieved 28 October 2014 from http://www.ers.usda.
    gov/data-products/sugar-and-sweeteners-yearbook-tables.aspx
34  American Sugar Alliance (2010), Submission to the United
    States International Trade Commission, Washington, DC,
    2 March 2010. Retrieved 16 February 2015 from http://www.
    usitc.gov/press_room/documents/testimony/131_034_009.pdf
35  Michael LaForgia and Adam Playford (2012), 'Wikileaks:
    Fanjuls among "Sugar Barons" Who "Muscled" Lawmakers
    to Kill Free Trade Deal', *The Palm Beach Post*, 2 January 2012.
    Retrieved 28 October 2014 from http://www.palmbeachpost.
    com/news/news/wikileaks-fanjuls-among-sugar-barons-who-
    muscled-l/nL2wg/
36  Robert Kuok made his fortune in sugar trading, hotel property
    development (often with his partners in the sugar trade) and
    Coca-Cola bottling plants among other ventures.
37  Mongabay (2011), 'Indonesian Sugar Producers Seek 500,000
    ha of Land Exempted from Moratorium', *Mongabay News*,
    23 June 2011. Retrieved 28 October 2014 from http://news.
    mongabay.com/2011/0623-sugar_indonesia.html
38  George Abbott (1990), *Sugar*, London: Routledge, p. 88.
39  Philip McMichael (2006), 'Peasant Prospects in the Neoliberal
    Age', *New Political Economy* 11(3): 407–18. Quote on p. 414.

4  EXPLOITING AND EXPELLING LABOUR

1  International Fund for Agricultural Development (2010), *Rural
   Poverty Report 2011*. Rome: IFAD, p. 233.
2  Donald W. Attwood (1992), *Raising Cane: The Political Economy
   of Sugar in Western India*, New Delhi: Oxford University Press.
3  Fernanda Ludmilla Rossi Rocha, Maria Helena Palucci Marziale
   and Oi-Saeng Hong (2010), 'Work and Health Conditions of
   Sugar Cane Workers in Brazil', *Revista da Escola de Enfermagem
   da USP* 44(4): 978–83.
4  Luis Henrique Rafael, cited in Patrick McDonnell (2008),
   'Human Cost of Brazil's Biofuels Boom', *LA Times*, 16 June
   2008. Retrieved 24 March 2015 from http://www.latimes.com/
   world/la-fg-biofuels16-2008jun16-story.html#page=1

5  Isabelle Guérin (2013), 'Bonded Labour, Agrarian Changes and Capitalism: Emerging Patterns in South India', *Journal of Agrarian Change* 13(3): 405–23.

6  Kamala Marius-Gnanou (2008), 'Debt Bondage, Seasonal Migration and Alternative Issues: Lessons from Tamil Nadu, India', *Autrepart* 2(46): 127–42.

7  See Natasha Schwarzbach and Ben Richardson (2015), 'A Bitter Harvest: Child Labour in Sugarcane Agriculture and the Role of Certification Systems', *UC Davis Journal of International Law and Policy*, forthcoming.

8  COVERCO and the International Labor Rights Fund (2005), 'Labor Conditions in the Guatemalan Sugar Industry', May 2005. Retrieved 26 January 2015 from http://www.laborrights. org/sites/default/files/publications-and-resources/guatemala_ sugar.pdf

9  Sue Carswell (2003), 'A Family Business: Women, Children and Smallholder Sugar Cane Farming in Fiji', *Asia Pacific Viewpoint* 44(2): 131–48.

10  Maria Luisa Mendonça, Fabio Pitta and Carlos Vinicius Xavier (2013), *The Sugarcane Industry and the Global Economic Crisis*, The Hague, Netherlands: Transnational Institute and Network for Social Justice and Human Rights, p. 16. Retrieved 28 October 2014 from http://www.tni.org/sites/www.tni.org/files/ download/sugarcane_industry-en-final.pdf

11  COVERCO and the International Labor Rights Fund (2005), 'Labor Conditions in the Guatemalan Sugar Industry'.

12  Isabelle Guérin (2013), 'Bonded Labour, Agrarian Changes and Capitalism: Emerging Patterns in South India', *Journal of Agrarian Change* 13(3): 405–23.

13  ActionAid (2013), *Sweet Nothings*, Chard, Somerset: ActionAid.

14  M. Osava (2011), 'Brazil: Women Workers Determined to Ride the Wave of Mechanisation', *IPS News*, 28 March 2011. Retrieved 30 March 2015 from http://www.ipsnews. net/2011/03/brazil-women-workers-determined-to-ride-the- wave-of-mechanisation/

15  Barbara Pini (2005), 'Farm Women: Driving Tractors and Negotiating Gender', *International Journal of Sociology of Agriculture and Food* 13(1): 1–12.

16  International Union of Food Workers (IUF) (2004), 'Women Workers in the Sugar Sector of the English-Speaking

Caribbean', IUF Discussion Paper, December 2004. Retrieved 28 October 2014 from http://www.iuf.org/sugarworkers/wp-content/uploads/2012/07/Women-Sugar-Workers-E-S-Caribbean.pdf

17  Nandini Gunewardena (2010), 'Bitter Cane: Gendered Fields of Power in Sri Lanka's Sugar Economy', *Signs* 35(2): 371–96.

18  International Sugar Organization (2013), List of Participants: 22nd International Seminar, Canary Wharf, London, 26–27 November 2013. On file with author.

19  Christian Aid (2005), *The Damage Done: Aid, Death and Dogma*, London: Christian Aid.

20  Ramenya Gibendi, Benson Amadal and John Shilitsa (2014), 'Why the Poor Kenyan Sugarcane Grower will Remain a Slave of the Millers', *The Daily Nation*, 22 June 2014.

21  Peter Wallsten and Tom Hamburger (2013), 'Sugar Protections Prove Easy to Swallow', *The Washington Post*, 7 December 2013.

22  Ben White, Saturnino M. Borras Jr, Ruth Hall, Ian Scoones and Wendy Wolford (2012), 'The New Enclosures: Critical Perspectives on Corporate Land Deals', *Journal of Peasant Studies* 39(4): 619–48.

23  Data from Brazilian Ministry of Work and Employment, cited in José Giacomo Baccarin, Regina Aparecida Leite de Camargo and João Victor Barretto Noguiero Ferreira (2014), *Boletim Ocupação Formal Sucroalcooleira Centro Sul* 51 (April). Retrieved 28 October 2014 from www.fcav.unesp.br/#!/departamentos/economia-rural/docentes/jose-giacomo-baccarin/boletin-ocupacao-sucroalcooleira-em-sao-paulo/boletins-2014

24  European Committee of Sugar Manufacturers (CEFS) (2014), CEFS Sugar Statistics 2013 web page. Retrieved 28 October 2014 from http://www.comitesucre.org/site/wp-content/uploads/2014/04/CEFS-Sugar-Statisitics-Inquiry-2013-FINAL-DRAFTv4.pdf

25  Illovo Sugar (2014), Integrated Annual Reports web page. Retrieved 28 October 2014 from http://www.illovosugar.co.za/investors/integrated-annual-reports

26  United States Department of Agriculture (USDA) Sugar and Sweeteners Background web page. Retrieved 28 October 2014 from http://www.ers.usda.gov/topics/crops/sugar-sweeteners/background.aspx#.U_TjA_ldUWI

27  Beate Zimmermann and Jürgen Zeddies (2002), 'International

Competitiveness of Sugar Production'. Paper presented at International Farm Management Congress, Arnhem, the Netherlands, 7–12 July 2002. Retrieved 24 March 2015 from http://ageconsearch.umn.edu/bitstream/7000/2/cp02zi02.pdf

28 Donald Mitchell (2005), 'Sugar in the Caribbean: Adjusting to Eroding Preferences'. *World Bank Staff Working Paper*, WPS3802, December 2005. Retrieved 24 March 2015 from http://elibrary. worldbank.org/doi/pdf/10.1596/1813-9450-3802; Ben Richardson and Pamela Richardson-Ngwenya (2013), 'Cut Loose in the Caribbean: Neoliberalism and the Demise of the Commonwealth Sugar Trade', *Bulletin of Latin American Research* 32(3): 263–78.

29 Haydn Lewis (2006), 'Farmers Angry Over British Sugar "Insult"', *The York Press*, 2 August 2006.

30 Deliveries are negotiated between Südzucker and the individual sugar beet growers' associations that make up the cooperative.

31 Constanza Vieira (2008), 'COLOMBIA: Sugar Workers Strike for Basic Rights', *Inter Press Service*, 7 October 2008. Retrieved 28 October 2014 from http://www.ipsnews.net/2008/10/ colombia-sugar-workers-strike-for-basic-rights/

32 Cindy Hahamovitch (2009), *No Man's Land: Jamaican Guestworkers in America and the Global History of Deportable Labor*, Princeton, NJ: Princeton University Press.

33 See US Code, Title 29, Chapter 8, Section 207. Retrieved 15 January 2015 from http://www.law.cornell.edu/uscode/ text/29/207

34 Dominican Today (2015), 'Economic Sectors Snub Dominican Republic's Push to Regularize Aliens', *Dominican Today*, 13 January 2015. Retrieved 15 January 2015 from http://www. dominicantoday.com/dr/local/2015/1/13/53888/Economic-sectors-snub-Dominican-Republics-push-to-regularize-aliens

35 Biofuel Watch Center and Repórter Brasil (2011), Assessment of Working Conditions in Sugarcane Production presentation, December 2011. Retrieved 28 October 2014 from http://iet.jrc. ec.europa.eu/remea/sites/remea/files/files/documents/events/ glass_working_conditions.pdf

## 5 EXPANDING AND EXHAUSTING LAND

1 War Anseeuw, Liz Alden Wily, Lorenzo Cotula and Michael Taylor (2011), *Land Rights and the Rush for Land*, Rome: International Land Coalition.
2 Survival International (2013), 'World Mental Health Day: Suicide Epidemic Ravages Guarani', *Survival International News*, 9 October 2013. Retrieved 28 October 2014 from http://www.survivalinternational.org/news/9632
3 Klaus Deininger and Derek Byerlee (2011), *Rising Global Interest in Farmland: Can it Yield Sustainable and Equitable Benefits?* Washington, DC: World Bank.
4 International Sugar Organization (ISO) (2012), 'Outlook of Sugar and Ethanol Production in Brazil', *ISO Market Evaluation and Statistics Committee* 15(5): 5.
5 Tongaat Hulett (2014). See www.thdev.co.za for an example of 'upmarket living'.
6 Roman Herre and Timothé Feodoroff (2014), *Case Dossier: Cambodia – Sugar Cane Plantations, Human Rights Violations and EU's 'Everything But Arms' Initiative*, Heidelberg, Germany: FIAN Germany.
7 European Commission (2014), Trade Policy web page. Retrieved 28 October 2014 from http://ec.europa.eu/trade/policy/
8 Matthew Tostevin (2009), 'UAE Firms Eye Zambian Farming Land – Minister', *Arabian Business*, 12 June 2009.
9 Quoted in *The Great Land Rush*, dir. Hugo Berkeley and Osvalde Lewat. Normal Life Pictures, 2012. Retrieved 19 January 2015 from http://www.whypoverty.net/video/land-rush/
10 US Embassy Cable (2009), 'A Spoonful of Chinese Sugar Sours US Investors in Mali', hosted in Public Library of US Diplomacy. Retrieved 19 January 2015 from https://www.wikileaks.org/plusd/cables/09BAMAKO104_a.html
11 Associated NGOs (2011), 'MIFEE Project Violates Human Rights: Joint Press Release', *West Papua Media Alerts*, 14 August 2011. Retrieved 28 October 2014 from http://westpapuamedia.info/tag/the-indonesian-forum-for-environment/
12 Gail Hollander (2008), *Raising Cane in the 'Glades: The Global Sugar Trade and the Transformation of Florida*, Chicago: University of Chicago Press.
13 African Development Bank (ADB) (no date), Executive

Summary of the Environmental, Social and Health Impact
Assessment of the Addax Bioenergy Project in Sierra Leone,
ADB report, pp. 2–18. Retrieved 28 October 2014 from
http://www.afdb.org/fileadmin/uploads/afdb/Documents/
Environmental-and-Social-Assessments/Addax%20
Bioenergy%20-%20ESHIA%20summary%20-%20
Final%20EN.pdf

14  M. Mekonnen and A. Hoekstra (2011), 'The Green, Blue and
Grey Water Footprint of Crops and Derived Crop Products',
*Hydrology Earth System Sciences* 15: 1577–1600.

15  Meena Menon (2013), 'Maharashtra Drought Man-Made:
Analysis', *The Hindu*, 3 April 2013.

16  Jason Clay (2004), *World Agriculture and the Environment:
A Commodity-by-Commodity Guide to Impacts and Practices*,
Washington, DC: Island Press, p. 166.

17  Akali Moses, Nyongesa Destaings, Neyole Masinde and
J. Miima (2011), 'Effluent Discharge by Mumias Sugar
Company in Kenya: An Empirical Investigation of Pollution of
River Nzoia', *Sacha Journal of Environmental Studies* 1(1): 1–30.

18  Jason W. Moore (2000), 'Sugar and the Expansion of the Early
Modern World-Economy: Commodity Frontiers, Ecological
Transformation, and Industrialization', *Review (Fernand Braudel
Centre)* 23(3): 409–33.

19  Toby Musgrave and Will Musgrave (2000), *An Empire of Plants:
People and Plants that Changed the World*, London: Cassell
Illustrated, p. 47.

20  Jason Clay (2004), *World Agriculture and the Environment:
A Commodity-by-Commodity Guide to Impacts and Practices*,
Washington, DC: Island Press, p. 166.

21  Moore (2000), 'Sugar and the Expansion of the Early Modern
World-Economy'.

22  International Sugar Organization (ISO) (2012), 'Outlook
of Sugar and Ethanol Production in Brazil', *ISO Market
Evaluation and Statistics Committee* 15(5): 10. www.iso.sugar.
org/Membus%20documents/2012/MECAS%2812%2905%20
-%20Outlook%20of%20Sugar%20and20%Ethanol%20
Production%20in%20Brazil%20-%20English-pdf

23  Samantha Pearson (2013), 'Brazil's CTC Acquires Taste for GM
Sugar', *The Financial Times*, 24 April 2013.

24  Geoff Tansey (2002), 'Patenting Our Food Future: Intellectual

Property Rights and the Global Food System', *Social Policy and Administration* 36(6): 575–92.

25  Center for Food Safety (2012), 'Comments on Final Environmental Impact Statement for Genetically Engineered Glyphosate Tolerant Event H7-1 Sugar Beets, Docket Number APHIS-2010-0047', 9 July 2012. Retrieved 28 October 2014 from http://www.centerforfoodsafety.org/files/rrsb-feis-comments-7-9-12.pdf

26  Syngenta (2014), Crops and Innovation: Sugar Cane web page. Retrieved on 28 October 2014 from http://www.syngenta.com/ global/corporate/en/products-and-innovation/key-crops/Pages/ Sugarcane.aspx

27  Nero Cunha Ferreira (2014), 'Bioenergy in Brazil', Presentation from Brazilian Ministry of External Relations. Retrieved 28 October 2014 from http://www.b2match.eu/system/ biomassworkshop2014bogota/files/1-3.pdf?1392106897

28  British Sugar (2012), '100 Years of UK Beet Sugar Industry: Strong Roots, Sustainable Future'. Outreach Booklet. Retrieved 28 October 2014 from http://www.britishsugar.co.uk/Files/100-Years-Beet-Sugar-Outreach-Booklet.aspx

29  Cosan (2012), *Cosan: Our Business, Challenges, and Opportunities*. São Paulo: Cosan.

30  European Biodiesel Board and six other trade associations (2012), 'About-Turn by EU Commission on Biofuels Policy Set to Decimate Biofuels Industry in the Midst of the European Economic Crisis', Press Release, 17 October 2012. Retrieved 2 February 2015 from http://www.epure.org/sites/default/files/ publication/nd5740a804-bed2-5a40.pdf

31  United States Environmental Protection Agency (EPA) (2010), 'Renewable Fuel Standard Program (RFS2) Regulatory Impact Analysis', EPA-420-R-10-066, February 2010. Retrieved 28 October 2014 from http://www.epa.gov/otaq/ renewablefuels/420r10006.pdf

32  European Commission (2012), 'Impact Assessment . . . Amending Directive 2009/28/EC', Commission Staff Working Document, SWD(2012) 343, Brussels, 17 October 2012. Retrieved 28 October 2014 from http://ec.europa.eu/ energy/sites/ener/files/swd_2012_0343_ia_en.pdf

33  Perrihan Al-Riffai, Betina Dimaranan and David Laborde (2010), 'Global Trade and Environmental Impact Study of

the EU Biofuels Mandate', Final Draft Report prepared for
the International Food Policy Institute (IFPRI), March 2010.
Retrieved 28 October 2014 from http://www.ifpri.org/sites/
default/files/publications/biofuelsreportec.pdf

34  Gail Hollander (2005), 'The Material and Symbolic Role of the
Everglades in US National Politics', *Political Geography* 24(4):
449–75.

35  Alfred Light (2010), 'Reducing Nutrient Pollution in the
Everglades Agricultural Area through Best Management
Practices', *Natural Resources & the Environment* 25(2).

36  Andy Reid (2014), 'Sugar Industry Accused of Dodging
Everglades Clean-Up Costs', *Sun Sentinel*, 15 June
2014.

37  FAO, IFAD, UNCTAD and the World Bank (2010), 'Principles
for Responsible Agricultural Investment that Respects Rights,
Livelihoods and Resources', Discussion Paper, 25 January
2010. Retrieved 17 February 2015 from http://siteresources.
worldbank.org/INTARD/214574-1111138388661/22453321/
Principles_Extended.pdf

38  In 2010, the CFS rejected the Principles on Responsible
Agricultural Investment, but in 2014, after negotiations had
strengthened the emphasis on small producers and water usage,
a revised version of these guidelines was accepted.

39  The Coca-Cola Company (2014), Sustainable Agriculture web
page. Retrieved 28 October 2014 from http://tccc-sr.dolodev.
com/in-our-company/healthy-communities/sustainable-
agriculture.html

6  A SWEETER DEAL FOR ALL?

1  André Drainville (1994), 'International Political Economy in the
Age of Open Marxism', *Review of International Political Economy*
1(1): 105–32.

2  Tom Metcalf (2012), 'Suedzucker Was Largest Sugar Producer
in 2011–12 Season', *Bloomberg News*, 19 July 2012.

3  Südzucker AG (2012), *Annual Report Südzucker AG 2011/12*,
Mannheim: Südzucker AG.

4  Associated British Foods PLC (2012), *Annual Report and
Accounts 2012*, London: ABF.

5  Tereos reported total comprehensive income of 283 million euros, with almost half its sugar revenues coming from outside France.

6  Ben McKay, Sérgio Sauer, Ben Richardson and Roman Herre (2014), 'The Politics of Sugarcane Flexing in Brazil and Beyond', *Transnational Institute (TNI) Think Piece Series on Flex Crops and Commodities* 4, September 2014, p. 5.

7  House of Lords EU Agriculture, Fisheries, Environment and Energy Sub-Committee (2012), EU Sugar Regime, Oral Evidence, 20 June 2012, p. 80. Retrieved 16 February 2015 from http://www.parliament.uk/documents/lords-committees/eu-sub-com-d/sugar/sugarevidencevolume1.pdf

8  The technology does remain at an immature stage. I am grateful to one reviewer for flagging up this rather humorous review of a smart-fork, designed to remind its users not to eat too quickly by vibrating in their mouths: 'If you're concerned that the vibrating feature might be disruptive at the dinner table, don't worry, it only goes off when you put it in your mouth. It's barely audible over the sound of it grinding the enamel off your teeth.'

9  Claude Fischler (1987), 'Is Sugar Really an Opium of the People?', *Food and Foodways* 2(1): 141–50.

10  Pierre Bourdieu (1984), *Distinction: A Social Critique of the Judgement of Taste*, London: Routledge.

11  David Millward (2013), 'Jamie Oliver Sparks Poverty Row after He Attacks Families for Eating Junk Food', *The Daily Telegraph*, 27 August 2013.

12  UNCTAD (2012), *Commodities and Development Report*, New York and Geneva, United Nations.

13  Timothy Morton (1998), *The Poetics of Spice: Romantic Consumerism and the Exotic*, Cambridge: Cambridge University Press.

14  Retrieved 17 February 2015 from http://bonsucro.com/site/in-numbers/

15  Based on 2013 data. See Jason Potts, Matthew Lynch, Ann Wilkings, Gabriel Huppe, Maxine Cunningham and Vivek Voora (2014), *The State of Sustainability Initiatives Review 2014*, London: International Institute for Sustainable Development, p. 284.

16  Secretariat of the Pacific Community (2013), 'Training Provides Platform for Capacity-Building on Organic Certification Systems', *Secretariat of the Pacific Community News*, 11 June 2013. Retrieved 28 October 2014 from http://www.2008.spc.

int/fr/links-and-resources/1284-training-provides-platform-for-capacity-building-on-organic-certification-systems-.html

17  The Paraguay cooperative Manduvira has been Fairtrade-certified since 1999 and organic-certified since 2004. Equal Exchange is not an alternative to Fairtrade then, but a stream within it.

18  David Harvey (2010), *The Enigma of Capital and the Crisis of Capitalism*, London: Profile Books.

19  Trade Union Congress (TUC), 'Positive End to Colombian Sugar Cane Cutters' Strike', *TUC Briefing*, 8 December 2008. Retrieved 28 October 2014 from http://www.tuc.org.uk/international-issues/countries/colombia/positive-end-colombian-sugar-cane-cutters-strike

20  Washington Office on Latin America (WOLA) (2012), 'Murder of Trade Unionist Underscores Fragility of U.S.–Colombia Labor Action Plan', *WOLA Publications*, 30 April 2012. Retrieved 28 October 2014 from http://www.wola.org/publications/murder_of_trade_unionist_underscores_fragility_of_us_colombia_labor_action_plan

21  Human Rights Watch (2009), 'Child Labor in Sugarcane Plantations in El Salvador Drops by 70%', *Human Rights Watch News*, 16 September 2009. Retrieved 28 October 2014 from http://www.hrw.org/news/2009/09/16/child-labor-sugarcane-plantations-el-salvador-drops-70

22  Center for International Environmental Law (CIEL) (2009), 'Bitter Harvest: Defending Communities in Nicaragua'. CIEL background information. Retrieved 28 October 2014 from http://www.newhavenleon.org/yahoo_site_admin/assets/docs/Nicaragua_background_info_CIEL_8-7-09-2_recd_11_09.31954717.pdf

23  Y-Vonne Hutchinson (2014), 'Sickly Sweet: Human Rights Conditions for Sugarcane Workers in Western Nicaragua'. La Isla Foundation report. Retrieved 23 March 2015 from https://laislafoundation.org/sickly-sweet-report/

24  Tony Weis (2007), *The Global Food Economy: The Battle for the Future of Farming*, London: Zed Books.

25  Lindsey Mulkins, Roger Samson, Emmanuel Yap, Amongo, Teodoro Mendoz and Ben Ramos (2000), 'From Sugarcane Monoculture to Agro-Ecological Village', *Low External Input and Sustainable Agriculture (LEISA) Magazine* 16(2), December.

26  International Sugar Organization (ISO) (2011), 'Niche Sugar Markets', *ISO Market Evaluation and Statistics Committee* 11(5): 1.

27  Cited in David Baker (2013), 'Post-Organic: Leontino Balbo Junior's Green Farming Future', *Wired*, 14 August 2013. Retrieved 24 March 2015 from http://www.wired.co.uk/magazine/archive/2013/08/features/post-organic

28  Miguel Altieri (1995), *Agroecology: The Science of Sustainable Agriculture*, London: Intermediate Technology Publications.

29  Peter Rosset, Raj Patel and Michael Courville (2006), *Promised Land: Competing Visions of Agrarian Reform*, Oakland, CA: Food First Books.

30  FAO data on indexed export and import values shows that Cuba has been running small agricultural trade deficits (by historical standards) since 2005.

31  Peter Rosset (2011), 'Food Sovereignty and Alternative Paradigms to Confront Land Grabbing and the Food and Climate Crises', *Development* 54(1): 21–30.

32  See Biofuel Watch Center and Repórter Brasil (2008), 'Brazil of Biofuels: Sugarcane'. Biofuel Watch report. Retrieved 28 October 2014 from http://reporterbrasil.org.br/documentos/brazil_of_biofuels_v3.pdf

33  Jonathan Watts (2014), 'Brazil's Landless Workers Movement Renews Protest on 30th Anniversary', *The Guardian*, Global Development, 13 February 2014.

34  South African Sugar Association (SASA) (2014), SASA Welcome web page. Retrieved 28 October 2014 from http://www.sasa.org.za/HomePage1.aspx

35  Iqra Qalam and Joshua Lumet (2012), 'The Failure of Land Reform in South Africa', *World Socialist Web Site*, 6 December 2012. Retrieved 19 January 2015 from http://www.wsws.org/en/articles/2012/12/06/land-d06.html

36  Michelle Loubon (2014), 'Ex-Caroni Workers Deliver Letter to PM: Battle for Land and Money', *Trinidad Express*, 20 January 2014.

37  Rutgerd Boelens, Mourik Bueno de Mesquita, Antonio Gaybo and Francisco Peña (2011), 'Threats to a Sustainable Future: Water Accumulation and Conflict in Latin America', *Sustainable Development Law and Policy* 12(1): 41–69.

38  Wendy Wolford (2003), 'Producing Community: The MST and the Land Reform Settlements in Brazil', *Journal of Agrarian Change* 3(4): 500–20.

# Selected Readings

*In chapter 1*, the introduction speaks to two sets of literature: one on the political economy of food and agriculture, and the other on the history of sugar. For further reading on the former, see Raj Patel, *Stuffed and Starved: Markets, Power and the Hidden Battle for the World Food System* (London: Portobello, 2007); Jennifer Clapp, *Food* (Cambridge and Malden, MA: Polity, 2012); and Tony Weis, *The Global Food Economy: The Battle for the Future of Farming* (London: Zed Books, 2007). For further reading on the history of sugar, the starting point has to be Sidney Mintz, *Sweetness and Power: The Place of Sugar in Modern History* (Harmondsworth: Penguin, 1986). Accessible introductions can be found in Elizabeth Abbott, *Sugar: A Bittersweet History* (London and New York: Duckworth Overlook, 2009); and Peter Macinnis, *Bittersweet: The Story of Sugar* (London: Allen & Unwin, 2003). For more on the expansion of sugar cane beyond the Atlantic, see Jock Galloway, *The Sugar Cane Industry: A Historical Geography from its Origins to 1914* (Cambridge: Cambridge University Press, 1989); Sucheta Mazumdar, *Sugar and Society in China: Peasants, Technology, and the World Market* (Cambridge, MA: Harvard University Asia Center, 1998); and Ulbe Bosma, *The Sugar Plantation in India and Indonesia: Industrial Production, 1770–2010* (Cambridge: Cambridge University Press, 2013).

*Chapter 2* looks at the consumption of sugar. For

information on the politics of processed food marketing in the United States, see Marion Nestle, *Food Politics: How the Food Industry Influences Nutrition and Health* (Berkeley and Los Angeles, CA: University of California Press, 2002). For a focus on the United Kingdom and a more Marxist perspective on marketing, see Ben Fine, Michael Heasman and Judith Wright, *Consumption in the Age of Affluence: The World of Food* (London: Routledge, 1996). The concept of a 'nutrition transition' is associated with the work of academic nutritionist Barry Popkin and his piece 'Nutritional Patterns and Transitions', *Population and Development Review* 19(1) (1993): 138–57. A political analysis of this phenomenon can be found in Corinna Hawkes, 'Uneven Dietary Development: Linking the Policies and Processes of Globalization with the Nutrition Transition, Obesity and Diet-Related Chronic Diseases', *Globalization and Health* 2(4) (2006). Some of the most important interventions in the sugar consumption debate have come from medical academics, namely John Yudkin, *Pure, White and Deadly: How Sugar is Killing Us and What We Can Do to Stop It* (London: Davis-Poynter, 1972); and Robert Lustig, *Fat Chance: The Hidden Truth about Sugar, Obesity and Disease* (New York: Hudson Street Press, 2013). These accounts tend to reduce politics to lobbying by big food companies. For a more sophisticated account of food and body politics that draws on Michel Foucault's work, see Julie Guthman and Melanie DuPuis, 'Embodying Neoliberalism: Economy, Culture, and the Politics of Fat', *Environment and Planning D* 24(3) (2006): 427–48.

*Chapter 3* looks at international trade relations and the dilemma that this creates for national governments that want to protect domestic producers at the same time as sourcing the cheapest sugar possible. For an overview of agricultural trade at the World Trade Organization from the political economy discipline, see Rorden Wilkinson and James Scott (eds), *Trade, Poverty, Development: Getting Beyond the WTO's Doha Deadlock* (London: Routledge, 2013); and from the legal discipline, see Fiona Smith, *Agriculture and the WTO: Towards a New Theory of International Agricultural Trade Regulation* (Cheltenham and Northampton, MA: Edward Elgar, 2009). On the international trade in sugar specifically, see Michael Fakhri, *Sugar and the Making of International Trade Law* (Cambridge: Cambridge University Press, 2014); A. C. Hannah and Donald Spence, *The International Sugar Trade* (Cambridge: Woodhead Publishing, 1996); and Ben Richardson, *Sugar: Refined Power in a Global Regime* (Basingstoke: Palgrave Macmillan, 2009). There are a number of articles that explore the way that the sugar industry has lobbied for trade protectionism, typically based on rational actor models. This is the case in José Alverez 'Sweetening the US Legislature: The Remarkable Success of the Sugar Lobby', *The Political Quarterly* 76(1) (2005): 92–9. The role of ideas and identity in sugar trade politics is given greater consideration in Michael Billig, 'The Interests of Competing Elites: Fighting over Protectionism and "Free Markets" in Philippine Sugar', *Culture and Agriculture* 29(2) (2007): 70–7. For insight on the political economy of sugar in China – an area seriously understudied – see Louis Augustin-Jean, 'China's Sugar under Globalization Forces: Market Structures and State Decision Making in the Context of Liberalization', in Louis Augustin-Jean and Bjorn Alpermann (eds), *The Political Economy of Agro-Markets in China* (Basingstoke: Palgrave Macmillan, 2013), pp. 103–25. The broader place of commodities like sugar in international development is addressed in Thomas Lines, *Making Poverty: A History* (London: Zed Books, 2008).

*Chapter 4* turns to the labour process and the methods

of exploitation used in different sugar industries. A good starting point for thinking about how the working life of labour is shaped by different market structures and systems of production is to look at a case study country over time. One helpful text here is Michelle Harrison, *King Sugar: Jamaica, the Caribbean and the World Sugar Economy* (London: Latin American Bureau, 2001). Another suitable text, this time offering a distinctly feminist analysis, is Nandini Gunewardena, 'Bitter Cane: Gendered Fields of Power in Sri Lanka's Sugar Economy', *Signs* 35(2) (2010): 371–96. In terms of the different types of exploitation, on child labour see Laura Baas, 'Children on Bolivian Sugar Cane Plantations' in G. K. Lieten (ed.), *Hazardous Child Labour in Latin America* (Amsterdam: Springer Netherlands, 2011), pp. 191–209; on indentured labour see Isabelle Guérin, 'Bonded Labour, Agrarian Changes and Capitalism: Emerging Patterns in South India', *Journal of Agrarian Change* 13(3) (2013): 405–23; and on forced labour see Siobhan McGrath, 'Fuelling Global Production Networks with "Slave Labour"? Migrant Sugar Cane Workers in the Brazilian Ethanol GPN', *Geoforum* 44 (2013): 32–43. In terms of the institutional forms taken by organized labour in the sugar industry, excellent studies can be found in Jason Hickel, 'Subaltern Consciousness in South Africa's Labour Movement: "Workerism" in the KwaZulu-Natal Sugar Industry', *South African Historical Journal* 64(3) (2012): 664–84; and Craig Jeffrey, 'Caste, Class and Clientelism: A Political Economy of Everyday Corruption in Rural North India', *Economic Geography* 78(1) (2002): 21–42. On the prospects for better labour regulation, see Salo Coslovsky and Richard Locke, 'Parallel Paths to Enforcement: Private Compliance, Public Regulation and Labor Standards in the Brazilian Sugar Sector', *Politics & Society* 41(4) (2013): 497–526; and on human rights for sugar workers and their descendants in the Dominican Republic, see Samuel Martinez, 'Allegations Lost and Found: The Afterlife of Dominican Sugar Slavery', *Third World Quarterly* 33(10) (2012): 1855–70.

*Chapter 5* considers land exploitation, and in particular the way that industrial capital has organized the production of sugar so that it resembles 'factories in the fields'. A key text here is David Goodman, Bernardo Sorj and John Wilkinson, *From Farming to Biotechnology: A Theory of Agro-Industrial Development* (Oxford: Basil Blackwell, 1987). This is also central to the concept of substitutionism discussed in chapter 2. The work of Jason Moore also considers the production of nature under capitalism and uses examples from the sugar industry to illustrate this, as in his article 'Sugar and the Expansion of the Early Modern World-Economy: Commodity Frontiers, Ecological Transformation and Industrialization', *Review: A Journal of the Fernand Braudel Center* 23(3) (2000): 409–33. Exploring similar themes from a political ecology perspective, another helpful text in breaking down the artificial human/nature divide is Gail Hollander, *Raising Cane in the 'Glades: The Global Sugar Trade and the Transformation of Florida* (Chicago: University of Chicago Press, 2008). A central aspect of working or exploiting the land is acquiring control of it in the first place. To this end, the rapid expansion in the planting of sugar cane and other fungible crops is discussed in Klaus Deininger and Derek Byerlee, *Rising Global Interest in Farmland: Can it Yield Sustainable and Equitable Benefits?* (Washington, DC: World Bank, 2011). For a more critical perspective, consult Jun Borras, Philip McMichael and Ian Scoones, 'The Politics of Biofuels, Land and Agrarian Change: Editors' Introduction', *Journal of Peasant Studies* 37(4) (2010): 575–92. Finally, for more on the agronomy of sugar cane and sugar beet and their environmental impacts, see Oliver Cheesman, *Environmental Impacts of Sugar Production: The Cultivation and Processing of Sugarcane and Sugar Beet* (Wallingford, Oxfordshire: CABI Publishing, 2004); and on the philosophy of agro-ecology see Miguel Altieri and Clara Nicholls, 'Agroecology Scaling Up for Food Sovereignty and Resiliency', *Sustainable Agriculture Reviews* 11 (2012): 1–29.

*Chapter 6* suggests how 'reform from below' could make sugar provisioning more ecologically sound and socially just. The analysis in this chapter is driven by the idea that these reforms spring from the contradictions of capitalism itself. This is drawn from James O'Conner, 'Capitalism, Nature, Socialism: A Theoretical Introduction', *Capitalism, Nature, Socialism*, 1(1) (1988): 1–38. The phrase 'ecologically sound and socially just' is taken from another eco-Marxist writer, Fred Magdoff, 'An Ecologically Sound and Socially Just Economy', *Monthly Review* 66(4) (2014, no page numbers). For further evaluation of the effectiveness of certification schemes in the sugar industry, see David Phillips, 'Uneven and Unequal People-Centered Development: The Case of Fair Trade and Malawi Sugar Producers', *Agriculture and Human Values* 31(4) (2014): 563–76, and Theresa Selfa, Carmen Bain and Renata Moreno, 'Depoliticizing Land and Water "Grabs" in Colombia: The Limits of Bonsucro Certification for Enhancing Sustainable Biofuel Practices', *Agriculture and Human Values* 31(3) (2014): 455–68. For older studies of appropriate technology, see Raphael Kaplinsky, *Sugar Processing: The Development of a Third World Technology* (London: Intermediate Technology Publications, 1984); and for newer methodologies of participatory video see Pamela Richardson-Ngwenya and Ben Richardson, 'Documentary Film and Ethical Foodscapes: Three Takes on Caribbean Sugar', *Cultural Geographies* 20(3) (2013): 339–56. Land reform across a diverse range of countries is discussed in Peter Rosset, Raj Patel and Michael Courville, *Promised Land: Competing Visions of Agrarian Reform* (Oakland, CA: Food First Books, 2006); and more detail on the experience of Cuba can be found in Brian Pollitt, 'The Rise and Fall of the Cuban Sugar Economy', *Journal of Latin American Studies* 36(2) (2004): 319–48. A sympathetic yet critical account of the MST with respect to settlement on sugar-cane land can be found in Wendy Wolford, 'Of Land and Labor: Agrarian Reform on the Sugarcane Plantations of Northeast Brazil', *Latin American Perspectives* 31(2) (2004): 147–70, while the adjustment by sugar millers to a post-Apartheid era in South Africa is surveyed in Henry Bernstein, 'Commercial Agriculture in South Africa since 1994: "Natural, Simply Capitalism"', *Journal of Agrarian Change* 13(1) (2013): 23–46.

# Index